DAILY PULSE
The rhythm of the Tao

Dr. Debra Ford Msc.D

Copyright © 2018 Dr. Debra Ford Msc.D
Author:
Dr. Debra Ford Msc.D, inspirational teacher and spiritual mystic
Editor:
John. C. Ford M, charismatic adventurer and intellectual lateral thinker

Publisher: Energy Mountain Inc.
    716 Brookpark Drive SW, Calgary, AB, Canada, t2w 2x4
    T: 403.998.0191
    E: **answers@SolePath.org**
    W: **www.SolePath.org**
    W: **www.DailyPulse.ca**

Library and Archives Canada Cataloguing in Publication

Ford, Debra, 1957-, author
        Daily Pulse
/ Dr. Debra Ford.

Issued in print and electronic formats.

ISBN 978-1-987975-20-8

    1. Self-realization.   2. Success--Psychological aspects.
    I.   Title.

DEDICATION

I started writing this book while on a visit to Hong Kong to see my son Joel and his wife Shirley in April 2018. They were expecting their first child, our first grandchild.

I dedicate this book to our beautiful Emilia Rose, born in July 2018, who has made her mark on me and our family.

Welcome beautiful one and thank you for choosing us to be in your life. You are deeply loved.

CONTENTS

ACKNOWLEDGMENTS

None of my books would be possible without the lessons learned from those who come to me for counseling and teaching. Deep gratitude to all of you. You help me live my purpose, because without you I would not be able to be my inspirational teacher and spiritual mystic SolePath.

Special thanks to Brenda for sharing her inspiring journey and her personal journal.

Deep abiding love to our team, the four core, who walk in sync with me and share this SolePath journey; John and I, Deneen and Terry living our life's purpose, making SolePath a reality.

PROLOGUE

Starting and ending each day with deliberate choices creates ritual in life in sync with the essential rhythm of nature. The Daily Pulse is a ritual that helps you to look past distress and confusion, to bring habits into everyday life that help you find peace and calm. The Daily Pulse is a daily ritual, small steps towards life transformation and happiness.

The Daily Pulse encourages you to see beyond the ache and disorientation of life's challenges, to bring normalcy and ritual to everyday. It reminds you of the gift of life. Life is a journey filled with ups and downs and there are sometimes dark moments that you are challenged to navigate. The Daily Pulse is for you if you are going through change; if you are feeling stuck and helpless; if your life feels as though it has no meaning; if you are experiencing any of life's challenges including divorce, a difficult medical diagnosis or grief.

When your normal coping mechanisms or spiritual tools are not working for you and you need help looking past the dark to see the light, the Daily Pulse is the ritual of doing something uplifting and positive for yourself every day.

Rhythm helps us cope with life. Even simple habits such as coffee or tea in the morning give life rhythm and bring stability and normalcy to each day. The Daily Pulse helps you navigate life's challenges and is part of a journey of deep self-awareness that leads to happiness.

The Daily Pulse puts you in sync with the Tao, the heartbeat of nature. The Tao is the essential rhythm of nature, the fundamental pulse of our world. The Daily Pulse reminds you that personal change happens in small steady steps each day. That transformation of how you feel, happens in the gift of time spent alone, in the ritual of an inner process.

The Daily Pulse brings ritual to life, a precious ordinary experience that reawakens you to the beauty of a single moment.

Section 1

looking past distress and confusion

One bird announces Spring.

One step changes everything.

1.1 THE DAILY PULSE

I t had been a year of struggle and adversity for Brenda; an exhausting time in her life with one challenge after another coming at her constantly, with no respite. It was twelve months of the perfect storm including a terrible medical diagnosis for a loved one, ill-health that touched all parts of her family, as well as tough times in her city that caused her to lose her job and affected her ability to sustain herself.

At first she felt that she was coping and holding it all together, but one day she woke up and knew that it was all too much for her. Her life had changed and she just didn't have the tools to cope anymore. Even the small things that she used to shrug off felt too big and she slowly but surely collapsed into fear energy, giving in to the worry and anxiety that had become her persistent and most familiar emotions.

Brenda knew that this wasn't healthy. She was trying to take care of herself, but it was harder and harder to find her place of peace, safety and contentment. She had a regular spiritual practice but it just wasn't working anymore. Her favourite and most effective positive metaphysical tools just weren't helping.

3

She was fast becoming an insomniac, lying awake night after night, uncertain how to cope with her sleep deprivation. Her tangled thoughts roaming from her anxiety about what she and her family were going through to wondering why the things that used to work for her – her spiritual tools – just weren't helping this time.

PERSONAL ENERGY

In our counseling sessions together we discussed energy, her personal energy. Brenda understood that every thought, every emotion, every life situation affected her personal energy. As with each of us, every day her energy was moving between expansion and collapse. Just like a balloon being inflated and deflated depending on what was going on inside of her and outside of her.

She understood that she had an energetic aura and that healthy energy normally expands eight to ten feet away from her body. This was her neutral energy and it expanded out in all directions - up, down, front, back. She had the mental picture of existing in the middle of her energetic balloon.

Brenda and I had discussed the fact that for all of us, life is a journey filled everyday with ups and downs. There were light and dark moments that she was challenged to navigate. In each moment of each day, her personal energy was changing as she responded to what was going on in her life; collapsed inwards towards her body and expanding outwards away from her body depending on what she was experiencing.

Her positive expanding energy could move out from her body as far as thirty feet. Her negative collapsed energy imploded onto her body. She could well imagine her balloon filling with air, being blown up when she was experiencing positive expanding energy. Conversely, her balloon felt popped, with all of the air escaping when she was experiencing negative collapsed energy, causing her energy to collapse onto her skin.

When Brenda was experiencing positive expanding energy, she felt good, she experienced positive emotions, she felt well.

She understood that all of the good things in life were only possible in positive expanding energy – including mental and physical health, happiness and success. She knew that this was when she was connected to source energy, to her higher self, to her innate wisdom. In positive expanding energy, she could think clearly, make good decisions, find solutions to problems that led to great outcomes.

The problem was, that it had been quite a while since she had felt anything close to a positive emotion. She couldn't shake her worry and anxiety and just didn't know how to find that good feeling within the experiences of her life. What she was going through felt too big and overpowered each moment.

She was in that all too familiar cycle of negative collapsed energy, where she felt bad and experienced negative emotions and where she also felt physically unwell. She just couldn't find her way out of her negative energy and because of this she felt disconnected from Source, from her higher self, from her innate wisdom. She couldn't think straight, she made bad decisions, she couldn't find solutions to her problems.

Brenda knew that she couldn't change the situation around her,

SolePath Energy Sphere

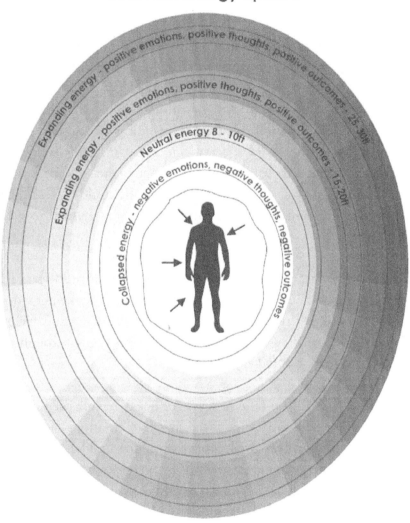

not the ill-health in her family, nor the recession in her city, but she understood that she needed to find a way to change the energy within herself.

We worked on two solutions - the power of her intention and rhythm and ritual - the Daily Pulse.

THE POWER OF INTENTION

IT IS ONLY ABOUT REACHING FOR A BETTER FEELING AND SOMETIMES A BETTER FEELING IS PEACE, CONTENTMENT, GRATITUDE.

AND SOMETIMES A BETTER FEELING IS SIMPLE SURRENDER, SIMPLE AWARENESS THAT WHAT I AM FEELING IS NOT WHO I AM AND WHERE I WANT TO BE.
SETH

Even on her worst day, there was one thing that Brenda could count on and that was her desire to feel better. She yearned, within this perfect storm to find a way to peace, calm and acceptance; to expanding energy.

Not to ignore what she was feeling, nor to diminish the experience of what she was going through, but to find ways to cope better with her life's challenges. She was struggling to actually feel better, but she certainly had the desire to feel better.

Brenda and I called this yearning to feel better, her intention. The desire and intention to feel better is powerful and expanding, in the same way that actually finding that good feeling is. The peace and acceptance around her struggles continued to evade her, but she was completely certain that she intended to feel better as soon as she was able.

Understanding the power of her intention started the process of mental and physical healing for Brenda. She began to feel empowered and knew that she was taking small steps towards leaving behind the helpless feeling of being buffeted by her life's challenges.

She couldn't change her outer world but she could change her inner world and this was the step forward that gave her confidence. The power of her intention to feel better gently started to reprogram her worry and anxiety about an unknown future.

Brenda needed everyday help and we created a daily ritual, a daily rhythmic program to further entrench her intention. She was ready to try look past the difficulties and sadness in her life and see the value that was there.

Ritual reminds us that personal change, coping with life's challenges, happens in small steady steps each day. Ritual reminds us that transformation of how we feel happens in the gift of time spent alone, in the rhythm of an inner process.

RHYTHM AND RITUAL

CEREMONY AND RITUAL HAVE THESE
PURPOSES:

RHYTHM, SANCTUARY, CONNECTION

WITH EACH OTHER AND WITH US.

SETH

Starting and ending each day with deliberate choices became a big part of creating calm for Brenda. Her daily ritual became a regular habit to provide rhythm and peace to her everyday life.

Ritual helps you take small steps towards life transformation, towards happiness. Ritual refreshes your awareness of life.

Now, is your point of creation. You don't create change in your life from the past nor from the future. Ritual brings you to the now, to the moment.

Ritual is a precious ordinary experience that reawakens you to the beauty of a single moment. Ritual helped Brenda remember that life is to be cherished, that she was safe and that she was not forgotten and most certainly was loved by spirit.

YOU ARE LOVED.
IT IS THE HUMAN EXPERIENCE TO
FORGET THIS.

IT IS OFTEN IN RITUAL THAT A
REMEMBERING OF THE LOVE OF GOD
OCCURS.

THIS IS IMPORTANT.
SETH

Brenda was already familiar with daily ritual. As a child, she had prayers and habits that were a big part of her growing up in a religious household; habits that sustained her through a very stormy childhood. The Daily Pulse seemed an easy daily ritual to integrate into her life.

She was ready to synchronize with the regular pulse of an insightful and uplifting ritual.

We have all experienced despair and other dark emotions. At one time or another, each and every one of us has lived through difficult experiences. This is a function of growing, evolving and being human.

In the chaos of life, it is possible to build upon your intention to feel better, your desire to feel different, even when you can't seem to find more positive emotions. In the chaos of life, it is possible to build upon your desire to find peace, calm and acceptance within

RITUAL IS LACKING FOR THOSE WHO
NO LONGER PARTICIPATE
IN THE RITUAL OF RELIGION.

IT IS NEEDED.

THE RHYTHM OF A PARTICULAR DAY FOR
REST, THE RHYTHM OF A PARTICULAR PLACE
THAT PROVIDES SANCTUARY;

A GATHERING TOGETHER WITH A COMMON
PURPOSE.
SETH

the struggle of your life experience, even when positive emotions seem appallingly remote.

Ritual encourages you to see beyond the ache and disorientation of the challenges of life and bring normalcy and rhythm to everyday. It reminds you of the gift of life as you create single peaceful moments.

Brenda committed to the Daily Pulse ritual to create rhythm, sanctuary and connection. She clung to this new ritual until, with ease, it started to work its magic and she found her feelings of love and safety slowly start to return.

The Daily Pulse is a ritual that helps you navigate life's challenges and is part of a journey of deep self-awareness that gently and naturally leads to happiness.

The Daily Pulse is built on the teachings of the Tao. The Tao is the heartbeat of nature, the essential rhythm of nature, the fundamental pulse of our world.

We need daily ritual and
ceremony to help us
understand ourselves better
and feel happier.
Dr. Debra

1.2 INTRODUCTION TO THE TAO

At the SolePath Institute, the Tao (pronounced Dow) is the foundation of all of our work. The Tao represents the fundamental nature of the universe, the origin, the creator. The Tao, loosely translated, means your path or your life's journey and is experienced by all.

The Tao cannot be accurately defined nor expressed in words. In this way it mirrors quantum mechanics, in that it can be observed and experienced, but never fully defined nor understood. In Taoism, Buddhism and Confucianism, the object of spiritual practice is to become 'one with the Tao', to synchronize with the pulse of nature, to allow and experience non-resistance.

The Tao is the natural order of the universe. The Tao keeps the world balanced and flowing. The Tao encompasses chi, the essential energy of 'all'.

The Tao is your being-ness, your deep knowing that you are more than your physical body and that the purpose of your life on earth is to make a difference. The Tao is accepting that you are here for only one reason – the evolution of your soul.

The Tao is the process by which the universe expresses itself and teaches that the only constant in life is change – change is about accepting movement in your life with ease, allowing for transformation, accepting your path, living in the 'now' and embracing the moment.

The Tao shows you that your life has seasons – spring, summer, autumn and winter; that there is a constant opening and closing of energy for all of us; that this is a natural unfolding process and that this is something to embrace – not to fear.

The key understandings of the Tao are

Connection – between us all and also with everything
Balance – when one part is out of balance, all parts are affected
Flow – non-resistance to what is going on around you

The Tao teaches that the fundamental law underlying everything in the universe is utterly plain and simple, no matter how complicated life may appear. The Tao is intrinsically connected to yin yang, the tai chi and to the eight original building blocks of nature called trigrams.

The Tao is accepting that you are here on earth for the evolution of your soul and this is accomplished through experiencing negative collapsed energy and then choosing positive expanding energy. Through experiencing life's challenges you find your place of peace and calm within them.

The eight trigrams of the Tao together form the yin yang, the tai chi.

Tai Chi

The eight trigrams of the Tao are called thunder and lake, mountain and wind, water and fire, earth and heaven and are made up of solid (yang) and broken (yin) lines:

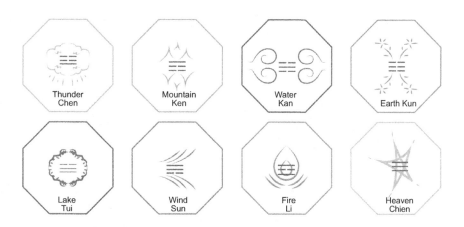

Your life becomes a process of accepting and working within the flow of positive expanding energy and negative collapsed energy; between the tai chi and the eight trigrams of nature. As you accept your soul's plan for this lifetime, your soul's desire for a life experience – you also understand that this planet that you live on is a creative environment and that with your free will you are creating your life.

Through the teachings of the Tao you deeply appreciate that you are more than your physical body and that we are all connected to each other. That when one part is out of balance, all parts are affected and that life is all about flow, about non-resistance and accepting.

1.3 CREATING CHANGE

Brenda knew that although she couldn't change what was going on around her – for her wellbeing and her mental and physical health, something had to change. The change had to be within her.

> THIS IS INDEED A TIME OF TRANSITION; A TIME OF MOVING FROM ONE PLACE OF EXPERIENCE TO A DIFFERENT ONE.
>
> THERE IS A VIBRATION CHANGE WITHIN YOU THAT IS ALTERING THE VIBRATION OF ALL OF YOU.
>
> SETH

It's sometimes helpful to look at the psychology of what you are going through; the textbook diagnosis of your very personal experience. It's good to understand that your response to life's difficulties is normal, usual and that others have had and are having similar experiences. It's part of not feeling so alone as you try to cope.

Let's take a look at the process of change. Most of us understand that creating change in life takes time, that we generally resist change and that change isn't easy.

Because change is difficult, we are generally only willing to change when we feel that we have no other option.

We are only willing to change when we feel painted into the proverbial corner; when we feel that our back is against the wall; when we know that we just can't live this way anymore.

Although discomfiting, this feeling of despair is actually a great moment. Strength grows in the moment you feel you can't go on in the same way, with the same life and this strength is the impetus for change.

Change can be painful, but you know at this stage, that nothing could be worse than staying in the same place, feeling the same unhappiness. The Tao teaches us that the only constant in life is change and we need to remember that resisting change is the source of our unhappiness.

STAGES OF CHANGE MODEL

There is a process that explains how conscious decisions to create change are made. The 'Stages of Change Model', developed by Prochaska and DiClemente in the late 1970's is still used by social workers, therapists and psychologists to understand behaviours and the process of change.

The Stages of Change Model assesses an individual's readiness to act, to create the change that they desire. Take a look at the six stages of change to determine how ready you may be to create transformation to feel happier.

Stage 1: Precontemplation – feeling overwhelmed about the situation, but not ready to take action. Not fully understanding the impact of negative thoughts, emotions and actions on your own life and the lives of others. Feeling stuck or helpless.

Stage 2: Contemplation – understanding that change is needed and intending to feel better. Desiring and yearning for change. Knowing that you can't stay where you are. Knowing that the state that you are living in is untenable; that something needs to be different.

Stage 3: Preparation – ready to take action and get help and advice – it could be reading a book, asking a counselor for help or joining a support group. Asking for help is a significant step towards feeling better as well as being determined that taking this step will have the desired effect.

Stage 4: Action – putting a plan into place, changing your behaviour and taking action to move forward with the intention to feel better. This is the critical stage for creating positive change in life. This is when Brenda introduced the Daily Pulse into her every day life.

Stage 5: Maintenance – keeping up with the plan and practice. Sustaining new healthy habits, implementing new tools, setting aside the time and being disciplined.

Stage 6: Termination – complete commitment to the new habit with no desire to return to the unwanted state. Creating a new paradigm for your life, a new way of being.

> CHOOSE JOY.
> PERHAPS TODAY YOU CAN CHOOSE
> TO FEEL SAFE. PERHAPS TODAY YOU CAN
> CHOOSE NOT TO RESIST.
>
> CHOOSE SOMETHING DIFFERENT, CHOOSE
> SOMETHING MORE POSITIVE;
>
> IT IS POSSIBLE.
>
> CONSCIOUSLY CHOOSING, DELIBERATELY
> CREATING A LIFE OF JOY.
> SETH

FINDING CONTEXT AND THIRD PARTY TALK

Brenda and I often spoke about the context for her life difficulties, taking a bigger picture view about what she was experiencing. If she believed that she was a perfect eternal soul having a life experience. If she believed that her life incarnation was about soul expansion and personal growth. If she believed that her soul had a plan that included all of her life experiences. Then she could also believe that there was nothing going on in her life that she couldn't cope with; that her soul was watching over her; that she was safe and all was going to be well.

One of the tools we introduced to help her navigate her trauma, as well as be a catalyst for the change she was intending, was to talk to herself in the third person. For example, when she felt the panic begin to set in, she asked "Why do you think Brenda is feeling panic?" instead of "Why am I panicking?" When she felt fear of what was happening overtake her, she asked "Why is Brenda afraid?" instead of "Why am I afraid?"

This technique evoked a completely different response from Brenda. She became the observer. She felt more detached from the situation and created distance for herself from her traumatic life experiences. The space she felt between herself and what was going on created separation for her from her collapsing negative emotions. Suddenly they didn't seem so overpowering and overwhelming.

In life, we often are able to give great advice to others when they are experiencing their troubles, but are just too close and emotionally entangled within ourselves to find solutions. We struggle to find solutions because we are disconnected from our wisdom when we are experiencing energetic collapse. Using this third person technique is almost as if you are asking loving objective questions of your best friend.

Using third person talk quickly became a way to manage Brenda's surges of overwhelming negative emotion and we introduced this technique into her Daily Pulse ritual.

Navigating life's ups and downs is a function of being human. Feeling positive and feeling negative are part of a normal life experience. What's different is how you choose to respond to those things that happen to you, that are outside of your control.

It is very easy to be a positive and happy person when things are going well, but who are you going to be when things aren't, when your life is filled with experiences that you don't want?

Brenda had enough desire and intention to find her way to peace and safety again. She was willing to move through the process of change. She took steps to introduce the Daily Pulse into her life and then she was willing to trust as the magic began.

1.4   WHAT IS THE DAILY PULSE

❖ Starting and ending each day with deliberate choices creates ritual in sync with the essential rhythm of nature.

❖ The Daily Pulse is a ritual that helps you look past distress
and confusion, to bring habits into everyday life that help
you find peace and calm.

❖ The Daily Pulse is a daily ritual; small steps each day towards life transformation and happiness.

❖ The Daily Pulse encourages you to see beyond the ache and
disorientation of life's challenges, to bring normalcy and
ritual to everyday. It reminds you of the gift of life.

❖ The Daily Pulse helps you navigate life's challenges and
is part of a journey of deep self-awareness that leads to
happiness.

❖ The Daily Pulse puts you in sync with the Tao, the heartbeat of nature. The Tao is the essential rhythm of nature,
the fundamental pulse of our world.

❖ The Daily Pulse reminds you that personal change happens
in small steady steps each day. That transformation of how
you feel, happens in the gift of time spent alone, in the
ritual of an inner process.

❖ The Daily Pulse brings ritual to life, a precious ordinary experience that reawakens you to the beauty of a single moment.

I have found in my metaphysical studies that the creation stories of the major religions that emanate from the Middle East - Christianity, Islam, Judaism - revolve around people and their relationship with God and with each other.

In eastern philosophy – Buddhism, Confucianism and Taoism - the creation story is about nature and how it interacts with itself. The trigrams of the Tao are the fundamental building blocks of nature and they have a pulse, a rhythm that has a profound impact on life.

The ritual of the Daily Pulse is based on the trigrams of the Tao. I was chatting through the foundational teaching of the Tao with my friend Barbara and she said that her favourite part of the Tao is that it doesn't need to be understood at an intellectual level, but rather experienced and felt at an emotional level. The Tao and the Daily Pulse are focused on emotions, on feeling better, on happiness.

The purpose of your Daily Pulse is to synchronize you with the Tao, the essential rhythm of nature, for the express purpose of being happier.

Your Daily Pulse brings you understandings and helps you make choices to facilitate change in your life.

Your Daily Pulse is nine steps of ritual, beating in synch with the pulse of the Tao.

THE SECRET TO A HAPPY LIFE ... THERE IS
ONLY ONE WAY TO DO THIS ... TO CHOOSE A
BETTER FEELING IN THE MOMENT.

TO CHOOSE TO FEEL BETTER RIGHT HERE,
RIGHT NOW.

IT IS THE REASON FOR YOUR EXISTENCE.

THIS IS THE PURPOSE OF YOUR LIFE.

ALL ELSE FLOWS FROM THIS
SETH

Your Daily Pulse helps you make happier choices for yourself and
for those around you.

IN EACH EXPERIENCE OF YOUR LIFE,
AS YOU DETERMINE YOUR FEELINGS,
TO MAKE CHOICES THAT CREATE A
BETTER FEELING.

THE ENERGETIC IMPACT OF THIS ON
YOUR PLANET IS HUGE; THE IMPACT ON
SELF IS HUGE; THE IMPACT ON
COMMUNITY IS HUGE.

SETH

Your Daily Pulse helps you deliberately create your life of joy.

THIS LIFE IS ONLY ABOUT JOY, YOU KNOW.

SOME LIVE LIVES OF JOY, NOT BECAUSE
ONLY JOYFUL THINGS HAPPEN TO THEM

BUT BECAUSE THEY ARE CAUTIOUS AND
DELIBERATE ABOUT THEIR RESPONSE TO
WHAT IS HAPPENING IN THEIR LIVES.

CONSCIOUSLY CHOOSING,
DELIBERATELY CREATING A LIFE OF JOY.
SETH

Your Daily Pulse is nine steps working through the Tao. You will be introduced to each trigram of the Tao and the light and dark energy that characterizes it. All parts of the light expanding energy can become part of your life with intention and conscious deliberate choice.

Although we will discuss all parts of the dark collapsed energy, and give you a full picture, there will likely be only one or two aspects that are showing up in your life and need to be worked on and you will be guided to focus on these.

DAILY PULSE RITUAL

Intention
Each day, guided by the Tao, you will set an intention for your Daily Pulse.

The Tao
will help you
make happier choices.

Dr. Debra

Breath prayer

You will participate in a guided breath prayer. A breath prayer is a wonderful way to bring you to the moment, to the 'now'. Seth teaches that you can only create your life from this moment; life is not created from the past nor from the future. Finding your way to happiness and light expanding energy can only be done from now and a breath prayer is a quick efficient way to bring yourself to this moment.

Journaling

You will journal. Journaling can take many forms including writing, drawing or scrapbooking. It is a way to record your experiences so that you can review them at another time and build on what you have learnt. Often journaling allows for insights that you may not receive if you don't take this creative time to reflect.

Your journaling will include writing a note to your higher self.

This can take the form of a prayer, an asking for help.

27

Asking higher self, your guides, your angels, your God, to create solutions, to intervene on your behalf.

Or it can take more of a meditative form, receiving wisdom and understanding, and clarity.

It could be a simple thank you to spirit, an exercise in gratitude.

It could also be asking higher self what your life would be like if you lived in light expanding energy.

Antidote and action

You will be given an antidote and action for each day. Ways to bring the light expanding energy of each trigram of the Tao into your life; action steps to be taken.

THE DAILY PULSE AND RHYTHM

Choose a time and place for your Daily Pulse ritual. A regular time, a gift to yourself, working on yourself.

Find a place that you can set up, perhaps as an altar with some items that have special spiritual significance for you. Perhaps simply a quiet chair where you can reflect and perform the meditative breath exercise and complete the journaling. Uninterrupted. This is your time for creating positive change in your life, for finding more happiness.

You won't need more than fifteen minutes each day, but you may like to spend more time than that. Make a commitment to a regular time of day. Practicing the Daily Pulse is a great way to start your day, to set the energetic tone for your day. Give yourself the opportunity to do a short review at the end of the day too.

Sometimes the daily exercise will really speak to you and the understandings that you receive will be profound. Sometimes the daily exercise may not seem to apply to you – but work through each of the nine steps to receive the full impact of the balance of the Tao in your life.

You could choose to focus on one trigram of the Tao each week, to revisit the lessons from one trigram for a consistent period of seven days. Or you could choose to move through a different trigram each day, and then go back to complete the cycle as many times a you need. Research suggests that it takes more than twenty one days to change a habit, so give yourself the time.

NOW! IT IS TRULY ALL THAT YOU HAVE.

BEING IN THE MOMENT IS THE SECRET TO HAPPINESS AND FULFILLMENT.

EVERY MOMENT IS A NEW BEGINNING.

SETH

THE DAILY PULSE AND BEHAVIOUR

Each of the eight trigrams of the Tao and the tai chi have an associated positive expanding energy and negative collapsed energy.

In any life situation, light or dark, positive or negative, when you are triggered, one of the trigrams of the Tao is being affected and your energy is responding in either a collapsed or expanding way.

Within the Tao, each negative collapsed energy has a positive expanding energy; a light reprogramming energy that assists with overcoming and changing the dark manifestation.

Your Daily Pulse, works through each trigram of the Tao and helps you understand what is happening to your emotions and gives you exercises and direction for finding happiness. You will gain deeper understanding of what triggers you and discover choices to find your happiness.

Through the teachings of the Tao you will know that what is happening to you, affects all of us and that when you are out of balance, we are all impacted. You will know that life is a choice and your choices affect your behaviour, which is how you impact others.

The Tao represents your connection, your balance and your flow.

THE DAILY PULSE AND GEMSTONES

As an option you may also choose to include gemstones into your Daily Pulse ritual. Each trigram of the Tao has a gemstone that matches its vibration. Each day a gemstone may be used to enhance the experience of the Daily Pulse.

Hold the gemstone in your hand while completing your breath prayer and carry it with you all day to remind you of the teachings for that specific trigram of the Tao. Tumbled gemstones are easy to carry in your pocket or in a pouch.

Gemstones are gifts from the earth and carry energy that you can tap into. For thousands of years, different cultures have used gemstones to remove mental, physical and spiritual energy blocks.

Gemstones are believed to have healing powers. They are calming and help you cleanse your personal energy. Gemstones transmit and store energy and each gemstone has an energy that is unique to it.

If you plan to include the gemstones as part of your nine step Daily Pulse, have them all on hand, ready to use, perhaps displayed on your altar.

Trigram of the Tao	Gemstone	Gemstone energy
Fire	Tigers eye	Tigers Eye helps recognize inner resources, accomplish goals, it is energizing and sparkly
Earth	Rose quartz	Rose quartz is all about compassion, peace, tenderness and healing
Lake	Natural quartz	Clear quartz holds and amplifies intentions, clears personal energy, promotes happiness
Thunder	Jade	Jade encourages harmonious relationships, eliminates negativity, promotes clarity
Heaven	Smoky quartz	Smoky quartz links to the highest realms, improves meditation and brings serenity
Water	Black onyx	Onyx increases personal power, builds vitality, assists with inner strength and helps with trusting heart
Mountain	Lapis lazuli	Lapis Lazuli assists with accessing universal knowledge, promotes connection
Wind	Amethyst	Amethyst brings good fortune, clears personal energy, promotes clear thinking and respect
Yin yang	Citrine	Citrine balances and heals, bringing the energy of the sun into life

BRENDA'S DAILY PULSE JOURNAL

IN EVERY MOMENT OF EVERY DAY, IN EVERY
SITUATION YOU ARE FACED WITH CHOICES.

ALL OF THESE CHOICES HAVE AN OUTCOME,
OR BEHAVIOUR.

THIS IS ONE OF THE FUNDAMENTAL
QUESTIONS 'WHO WILL I BE IN RELATION
TO WHAT IS GOING ON AROUND ME?'

EVERY THOUGHT, FEELING, ACTION IS A
CHOICE.
SETH

There is a copy of Brenda's Daily Pulse journal in the appendix. An example of how she used the process and guidance, in the upcoming Section 2, to reach her own deep insights and understandings.

WHEN YOU LIVE YOUR LIFE
IN A PLACE OF
EXPANDING ENERGY

YOU PROTECT YOURSELF
ENERGETICALLY.

Dr. Debra

Section 2

your daily pulse – rhythm and ritual of the trigrams of the tao

2.1 YOUR DAILY PULSE – FIRE ENERGY

Fire
Li

UNDERSTANDING OF THE TAO

> The Tao shows you that your
> life has seasons -
> spring, summer, autumn and winter;
> that there is a constant opening and
> closing of energy for all of us;
> that this is a natural unfolding
> process;
> and that this is something to embrace
> - not to fear.
> Dr. Debra

TRIGRAM OF THE TAO – FIRE

When light and expanding, fire energy represents growth and charisma and is clear, warm, bright and enlightened.

When dark and collapsed, fire energy is too hot, explosive, destructive and can't exist alone; fire needs something to burn on.

Light expanding fire energy:

It's mesmerizing to look at a fire isn't it? Whether its sitting inside on a cold night, feeling the comfort of a warm fire or outside around a campfire, enjoying the uniqueness of being in the circle of light that keeps the dark away. Watching the flames dance and expand, reaching up and then falling down. Sometimes seeing pictures in the fire. Sometimes succumbing to the hypnosis of the flames.

Light expanding fire energy is part of your life on those days when you feel really clear about yourself and your life; when you have the courage to be yourself on a unique journey of personal growth and self-development. Light expanding fire energy reflects as independence, confidently living to the beat of your own drum, walking your own path.

Light expanding fire energy shows up when you are open-minded and enlightened. It shows up when you are approachable and responsive to the suggestions of others. It is also there when you lead by example and by the way you live your life.

You can sense light expanding fire energy within yourself when you get noticed in a crowd; when you shine and others are naturally drawn to you. Light expanding fire energy makes you feel bright and aware, remarkable and thoughtful.

One of the most beautiful things about fire energy is that it takes the smallest flame to light a space. A huge darkened room, can be changed by a small flame. In life it doesn't take much light expanding fire energy to have a wonderful impact on others. The smallest spark can rekindle the light in others. A brightness within you makes others feel good about themselves, with simple daily interactions that are warm and friendly.

Dark collapsed fire energy:

Yet, you also know that fire energy can be too hot and explosive. A fire out of control is terrifying in its destruction.

One of the most interesting characteristics of fire energy is that it can't exist alone, it always needs something to burn on. In your life, when you are experiencing dark collapsed fire energy – you are always impacting others in a destructive way. You don't exist alone. This could show up in your closest relationships as selfish and destructive behaviour with those you love. It could also show up in your daily interactions with perfect strangers as arrogance, unfriendliness, lack of consideration and closed mindedness.

Within yourself, dark collapsed fire energy makes you feel that the world is a dangerous place and you feel afraid. Those times when you feel small and are filled with apprehension and fear; when you expect disaster and catastrophe; when you lack courage – you are experiencing the dark energy of fire.

In your life, dark collapsed fire energy is also showing up when you jump to negative conclusions. When you make, with very little evidence, negative assumptions about situations and about people.

The only thing we can be certain of in life, is change. Change creates growth and growth is positive, yet most often, we resist change. Anytime you fear change, are resistant to anything new, or are just being stubborn – these are all examples of the dark energy of fire in your life.

An inability, or no desire, to stand alone. Being too dependent on others. Making demands of others. All signs of the dark energy of fire.

Dark collapsed fire energy can show up as a belief that when your body dies, your consciousness dies with it. A belief that your existence is dependent on your body and your experience of your body.

YOUR DAILY PULSE

Intention

In your journal, write this intention for the fire Daily Pulse:

> *My intention is to live in the light expanding energy of fire; to live as a clear, warm, bright and enlightened person who has courage and leads by example.*

Breath prayer

Find a comfortable sitting position, rest your hands in your lap or hold them by your heart. Close your eyes gently, feel your scalp and forehead soften.

Breathe in and breathe out, imagine that you are inside a shell, like the shell of an egg, and place your focus on this safe, exterior covering.

Quietly and to yourself, state this affirmation:

> *"I am charismatic and I am bright and aware and I choose to be true to myself."*

Breathe in and breathe out and quietly and to yourself state:

> *"I reprogram myself towards the light expanding energy of fire and I breathe in growth and I breathe out fear. I breathe in courage and I breathe out feeling small."*

Continue with soft breathing and say a quiet thank you for who you are, exactly as you are.

Journaling

Review the section on the light expanding energy of fire. All parts of the light expanding energy can become part of your life with intention and conscious deliberate choice. Write today's answers to these questions in your journal.

Q: What happens in your life when you allow yourself to shine, when you feel bright and aware?

Q: What does your journey of personal growth and self development look like?

Q: Do you have courage? Courage to be yourself, courage to be independent, courage to walk your own path?

Q: How do you interact with others? Are the words - open-minded, enlightened, approachable, responsive, thoughtful - part of your interactions?

Review the section on the dark collapsed fire energy and using the technique of third party talk answer the questions below.

Although we have covered all parts of the dark collapsed energy, there are likely only one or two aspects that are showing up in (insert your first name e.g. Brenda's) life right now. Focus on these.

Q: Which part of dark collapsed fire energy is (Brenda) experiencing now? How does it show up, where and with whom?

Q: What would (Brenda's) life be like if this could turn around and reprogram towards the light expanding energy of fire?

Write a note to your higher self.

Dear higher self …

This can take the form of a prayer, an asking for help. Asking higher self, your guides, your angels, your god, to create solutions, to intervene on your behalf.

Or it can take more of a meditative form, an asking for wisdom and understanding, for clarity.

It could be a simple thank you to spirit, an exercise in gratitude.

It could also be asking higher self about what your life would be like if you lived in light expanding fire energy.

Antidote and action

As an antidote to dark collapsed fire energy and to bring light expanding fire energy and the profound teachings of the Tao into your life:

> ➤ Connect with others by sharing your light.
> ➤ Balance your life by focusing on your personal growth and individual development.
> ➤ Find flow and non-resistance by consciously not making assumptions about what others are doing, thinking or feeling. Let them be.

Write down the action you will take to implement this antidote and manifest connection, balance and flow of the fire trigram.

GEMSTONE

Gemstones are gifts from the earth and carry energy that you can tap into. The gemstone for fire energy is Tigers Eye.

Tigers Eye helps you recognize your inner resources and inner strength.

Tigers Eye assists with accomplishing goals.

Tigers Eye is energizing and sparkly.

A SIMPLE DESIRE,

FOLLOWED BY A POSITIVE ACTION,

TO MAKE SOMEONE ELSE FEEL BETTER,

IS WHAT YOU ARE CALLED TO DO.

SETH

SUMMARY:

Light expanding fire energy

Fire: growth and charisma; clear, warm, bright and enlightened.

Intention for Fire: to live in the light expanding energy of fire; to live as a clear, warm, bright and enlightened person who has courage and leads by example.

Affirmation: I am charismatic and I am bright and aware and I choose to be true to myself.

Reprogramming: I reprogram myself towards the light expanding energy of fire and I breathe in growth and I breathe out fear. I breathe in courage and I breathe out feeling small.

Antidote: share your light with others; focus on individual development and personal growth; consciously stop making assumptions about what others are doing, thinking or feeling. Let them be.

2.2 YOUR DAILY PULSE
– EARTH ENERGY

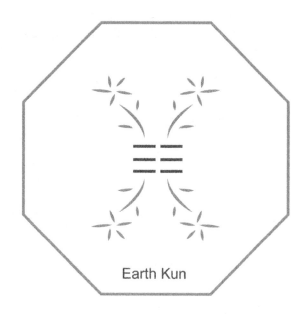

Earth Kun

UNDERSTANDING OF THE TAO

The Tao teaches that the
fundamental law underlying
everything in the universe is

utterly plain and simple,

no matter how complicated
life may appear.
Dr. Debra

TRIGRAM OF THE TAO – EARTH

When light and expanding, earth energy represents self-love and cherishing and is life giving and nourishing.

When dark and collapsed, earth energy absorbs too much and can't replenish itself.

Light expanding earth energy:

Isn't the energy of earth, the life giving beauty of our planet incredible? Somehow it's just too easy to forget that without our planet Earth, without earth energy none of us would exist. Earth energy sustains us; provides us with food, air and water. Earth energy provides us with the opportunity to make the soul choice to have an incarnation on this planet.

Light expanding earth energy is part of your life on those days when you feel nourished and able to nourish others.

When you are able to cherish and feed yourself mentally, physically and spiritually and this allows you to be nourishing to others. It starts with respecting yourself and feeling worthy of making yourself a priority.

Light expanding earth energy shows up when you give and receive love easily; when you effortlessly connect with others; when you feel that you belong. And all of this is happening while you keep your sense of self.

Earth energy provides life. Earth energy provides transformation. Earth energy provides opportunity for your soul evolution. Earth energy helps you understand that you need to take care of yourself first; put on your own oxygen mask before helping anyone else.

The trigram of the Tao for earth is three broken lines, three yin lines. Yin energy is receptive, still and tranquil.

Dark collapsed earth energy:

Yet, you also know that earth energy can absorb too much and has difficulty replenishing itself. Earth gives and gives and gives and then needs nourishment - composting and watering, to replenish.

One of the most interesting characteristics of earth energy is that it is interdependent. It exists within symbiotic relationships with plants, within the natural cycle of life and death and giving and replenishing. In your life, when you are experiencing dark collapsed earth energy –you are negatively impacting yourself. The cycle is unbalanced, you are giving too much and not receiving enough nourishment in return.

Within yourself, dark collapsed earth energy makes you feel that you don't matter and are unworthy. You feel inadequate, unhappy, unimportant and undeserving. You feel that it doesn't matter that your interactions with others are not balanced – too much giving and not enough receiving; when you feel that the needs of others take priority over your own.

In your life, dark collapsed earth energy is justified by waiting for 'heaven's reward', by sacrificing yourself now to gain future benefit and blessings. It is justified by living in self denial and then using this to keep score in your relationships. Dark collapsed earth energy is pernicious as you are sure that what you feel is true. You use emotional reasoning to justify situations regardless of their negative impact on you.

Anytime you have negative feelings about yourself; when you are being too hard on yourself; when you feel constantly disappointed, or overly sensitive to criticism – these are all examples of the dark energy of earth in your life. Light expanding earth energy is all about feeling worthy and feeling good about yourself.

Other signs of the dark energy of earth are a desperate desire to belong, looking for someone to 'complete' you or losing yourself in your relationships.

For some, dark collapsed earth energy can show up as a belief that you are helpless because you are at the mercy of events from past lives; other incarnations over which you now have no control. You feel that you must be punished, or you punish yourself for unkindness's done to others in past lives. You feel that you must accept the negative aspects of your life because of this supposed karma.

Intention

In your journal write this intention for the earth Daily Pulse:

> *My intention is to live in the light expanding energy of earth; to live as a nourishing and nourished person who keeps a sense of self in relationships.*

Breath prayer

Find a comfortable sitting position, rest your hands in your lap or hold them by your heart. Close your eyes gently, feel your scalp and forehead soften.

Breathe in and breathe out, place your focus and attention on the top of your head.

Quietly and to yourself, state this affirmation:

> *"I know who I am. I am important and significant and I choose to feel valued."*

Breathe in and breathe out and quietly and to yourself state:

> *"I reprogram myself towards the light expanding energy of earth and I breathe in worthiness and I breathe out unworthiness. I breathe in nourishment and I breathe out sacrifice."*

Continue with lovely soft breathing and say a quiet thank you for who you are, exactly as you are.

Journaling

Review the section on the light expanding energy of earth. All parts of the light expanding energy can become part of your life with intention and conscious deliberate choice. Write today's answers to these questions in your journal.

> Q: Is it as easy for you to nourish yourself, as it is to nourish others? Why is that?

> Q: What might change in your life if you did 'put on your oxygen mask first'?

> Q: How would your life feel if you did give and receive love easily, effortlessly connect with others and feel a deep sense of belonging?

> Q: What could you allow into your life to experience more of the light expanding energy of earth – for yourself and for others?

Review the section on the dark collapsed earth energy and using the technique of third party talk answer the questions below.

Although we have covered all parts of the dark collapsed energy, there are likely only one or two aspects that are showing up in (insert your first name e.g. Brenda's) life right now. Focus on these.

> Q: Which part of dark collapsed earth energy is (Brenda) experiencing now? How does it show up, where and with whom?

Q: What would (Brenda's) life be like if this could turn around and reprogram towards the light expanding energy of earth?

Write a note to your higher self.

Dear higher self ...

This can take the form of a prayer, an asking for help. Asking higher self, your guides, your angels, your god, to create solutions, to intervene on your behalf.

Or it can take more of a meditative form, an asking for wisdom and understanding, for clarity.

It could be a simple thank you to spirit, an exercise in gratitude.

It could also be asking higher self about what your life would be like if you lived in light expanding earth energy.

Antidote and action

As an antidote to dark collapsed earth energy and to bring light expanding earth energy and the profound teachings of the Tao into your life:

> Connect with others by allowing them to nourish you; and by nourishing them.
> Balance your life by focusing on your self love and who you are.
> Find flow and non-resistance by consciously choosing not to be so hard on yourself and making a choice not to be over sensitive to perceived criticism.

Write down the action you will take to implement this antidote and manifest connection, balance and flow of the earth trigram.

GEMSTONE

Gemstones are gifts from the earth and carry energy that you can tap into. The gemstone for earth energy is Rose Quartz.

Rose Quartz helps you show yourself and others compassion.

Rose Quartz helps you find peace and tenderness.

Rose Quartz assists with emotional healing.

KIND WORDS,
TO FRIENDS AND TO STRANGERS.

DELIBERATE ACTIONS WITH INTENT,
FOR POSITIVE CHANGE.

SETH

SUMMARY:

Light expanding earth energy

Earth: self-love and cherishing; life giving, nourishing

Intention for Earth: to live in the light expanding energy of earth; to live as a nourishing and nourished person who keeps a sense of self in relationships.

Affirmation: I know who I am, I am important and significant and I choose to feel valued.

Reprogramming: I reprogram myself towards the light expanding energy of earth and I breathe in worthiness and I breathe out un-worthiness. I breathe in nourishment and I breathe out sacrifice.

Antidote: nourish yourself and others; understand who you are and focus on self-love; make a choice not to be oversensitive to perceived criticism.

2.3   YOUR DAILY PULSE
- LAKE ENERGY

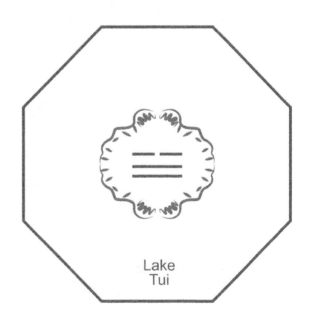

Lake
Tui

UNDERSTANDING OF THE TAO

The Tao represents
the fundamental nature of the
universe,
the origin, the creator.

The Tao, loosely translated,
means your path
or your life's journey,
and is experienced by all.
Dr. Debra

TRIGRAM OF THE TAO – LAKE

When light and expanding, lake energy represents positivity and communication and is joy; depth without overflowing.

When dark and collapsed, lake energy is stagnant.

Light expanding lake energy:

When I think of lake energy, I get this mental image of a beautiful small lake, surrounded on one side by trees, with a grassy verge on the other side. I see deer coming down for water. There are fish making ripples in the water; bugs skimming the surface. The lake is clear and reflects the sunlight. Birds are singing and everything seems right. I imagine an underground stream feeding the lake and keeping the water fresh, flowing and alive.

Light expanding lake energy is part of your life on those days when you feel positive, optimistic and engage in life as a 'glass half full' person; someone who knows deep in their core that life will work out.

Light expanding lake energy shows up when you feel playful, childlike and are having fun; when you are full of ideas and imagination. It show up when you are creative and expressive; when you bring fun and happiness into your life and the lives of those around you.

You know that light expanding lake energy is within you when life is lived in moderation, not overflowing and frantic. When your happiness has depth, is lasting and is real.

Light expanding lake energy supports great communication. It supports the ability to clearly communicate with others; to relate, connect and reach out to others in your life. It supports you as a team player who is loved and sought out by others.

Dark collapsed lake energy:
Yet when I think of dark collapsed lake energy, the image that I see is a lake in the shadows. No sunlight, no movement on or in the water. This lake is polluted, has too much algae, it is stagnant and sustains nothing.

Something is very wrong. Dark collapsed lake energy makes you feel that you don't matter and you are wrong. You don't fit in. You are in the wrong body. You are in the wrong family. You are in the wrong life. Something is not normal and just wrong.

Within yourself, dark collapsed lake energy causes you to dwell on the dark and negative and filter out any of the positives. You feel pessimistic and make a conscious and deliberate effort to stay focused on the negative side of people and events, even in the light of proof positive.

In your life, dark collapsed lake energy also encourages a false belief that you need to change to suit others; that others need to change to suit you; that life is wrong, if someone or something doesn't change.

Dark collapsed lake energy gives rise to being moody and indulging in self sabotage. You become closed to the flow of possibilities in life, sinking into stagnation.

Dark collapsed lake energy encourages a lack of communication and a deliberate creation of misunderstandings with those around you. You could be over eager to please others and become superficial, fake and frivolous. It also makes you too serious, which is often the result of having too much responsibility, too young.

For some, dark collapsed lake energy can show up as a belief that you are helpless because your personality and character were formed in infancy; through your genetics. You feel you are at the mercy of your genes and your past.

YOUR DAILY PULSE

Intention
In your journal write this intention for the lake Daily Pulse:

My intention is to live in the light expanding energy of lake; to live as a positive, full and fun person who is creative and full of ideas and imagination.

Breath prayer

Find a comfortable sitting position, rest your hands in your lap or hold them by your heart. Close your eyes gently, feel your scalp and forehead soften.

Breathe in and breathe out, place your focus and attention on your solar plexus, your core, your gut.

Quietly and to yourself state this affirmation:

> *"I am intuitive and I am fun and full and I choose to have fun."*

Breathe in and breathe out and quietly and to yourself state:

> *"I reprogram myself towards the light expanding energy of lake and I breathe in positivity and I breathe out pessimism. I breathe in happiness and I breathe out negativity."*

Continue with lovely soft breathing and say a quiet thank you for who you are, exactly as you are.

Journaling

Review the section on the light expanding energy of lake. All parts of the light expanding energy can become part of your life with intention and conscious deliberate choice. Write today's answers to these questions in your journal.

Q: What does a 'glass half full' life look like to you?

Q: If you could find a more positive frame of mind, what would be possible?

Q: How do you engage in life? Are you playful and fun? Creative and expressive? Do you bring happiness to yourself and those around you?

Q: How could better communication make your life easier and happier?

Review the section on the dark collapsed lake energy and using the technique of third party talk answer the questions below.

Although we have covered all parts of the dark collapsed energy, there are likely only one or two aspects that are showing up in (insert your first name e.g. Brenda's) life right now. Focus on these.

Q: Which part of dark collapsed lake energy is (Brenda) experiencing now? How does it show up, where and with whom?

Q: What would (Brenda's) life be like if this could turn around and reprogram towards the light expanding energy of lake?

Write a note to your higher self.

Dear higher self ...

This can take the form of a prayer, an asking for help. Asking higher self, your guides, your angels, your god, to create solutions, to intervene on your behalf.

Or it can take more of a meditative form, an asking for wisdom and understanding, for clarity.

It could be a simple thank you to spirit, an exercise in gratitude.

It could also be asking higher self about what your life would be like if you lived in light expanding lake energy.

Antidote and action

As an antidote to dark collapsed lake energy and to bring light expanding lake energy and the profound teachings of the Tao into your life:

> ➢ Connect with others by making time for fun together.
> ➢ Balance your life by focusing on clear, honest direct communication.
> ➢ Find flow and non-resistance by consciously choosing not to be so serious and pessimistic.

Write down the action you will take to implement this antidote and manifest connection, balance and flow of the lake trigram.

GEMSTONE

Gemstones are gifts from the earth and carry energy that you can tap into. The gemstone for lake energy is Natural or Clear Quartz.

Clear Quartz hold and amplifies intention.

Clear Quartz clears your personal energy.

Clear Quartz promotes happiness.

WHEN YOU SAY THAT THIS OTHER PERSON
CAUSED MY NEGATIVE THOUGHT OR FEELING,
YOU ARE ACTUALLY SAYING THAT I HAVE
FORGOTTEN
THAT I HAVE A CHOICE AROUND THIS.

THEY CAUSED THIS AND THEREFORE ARE
RESPONSIBLE FOR MY BEHAVIOUR.

THEREFORE MY NEGATIVE IMPACT ON 'WE' AND
'US'
IS NOT BECAUSE OF ME.

I FORGOT THAT I HAD A CHOICE.
SETH

SUMMARY:

Light expanding lake energy

Lake: positivity and communication; joy, depth without overflowing

Intention for Lake: to live in the light expanding energy of lake; to live as a positive, full and fun person who is creative and full of ideas and imagination.

Affirmation: I am intuitive and I am fun and full and I choose to have fun.

Reprogramming: I reprogram myself towards the light expanding energy of lake and I breathe in positivity and I breathe out pessimism. I breathe in happiness and I breathe out negativity.

Antidote: Make time for fun; focus on clear honest direct communication; consciously choose not to be so serious and pessimistic.

2.4   YOUR DAILY PULSE
– THUNDER ENERGY

Thunder
Chen

UNDERSTANDING OF THE TAO

The Tao cannot
be accurately defined

nor expressed in words,

it can only be observed
and experienced.

Dr. Debra

TRIGRAM OF THE TAO – THUNDER

When light and expanding, thunder energy represents power and connection; it denotes release and heralds nourishment.

When dark and collapsed, thunder energy is abrupt, loud, too powerful and chaotic.

Light expanding thunder energy:

Thunder energy is so interesting to me. It is powerful but doesn't have any of the destructive qualities of lightening. Like a trumpeter announcing the coming of the king, thunder is a powerful forerunner.

Thunder is a cleansing moment; is loud and announces that

restorative rain is coming. Thunder on a hot summer's day also reminds us that change happens when we least expect it.

The sound of thunder is said to be god's laughter. When wild swans rise up to fly together, the sound of their wings is like thunder.

Light expanding thunder energy is part of your life on those days when you feel powerful, but understand how to use this power in a way that is accepting of others. Light expanding thunder energy doesn't force situations and reinforces strong, safe, healthy connections with others.

Light expanding thunder energy shows in your deep desire to leave the world a better place, your yearning to be of service. You are inspiring to others by who you are and the way you live your life. You are looked up to as a role model.

You can see light expanding thunder energy when you are making things happen, bringing order and structure to situations; when you are able to see the outcome and the big picture.

In life, thunder is loud and sudden, yet completely non-judgmental. It is tolerance that sees both the positives and negatives in situations; not judging, but rather seeing what is needed.

Dark collapsed thunder energy:
Yet, you also know that thunder energy can be too powerful, chaotic, abrupt and loud. Thunder can cause fear. It can be seen as a harbinger of more frightening lightening or rain that is too much. Thunder is invisible, but it is certainly noticeable.

Within yourself, dark collapsed thunder energy makes you feel that the world is a dangerous place and you are unsafe; you feel at risk for harm or injury. Those times when you tend towards extreme negative generalizations about the safety of your life and the world – you are experiencing the dark energy of thunder.

In your life, dark collapsed thunder energy is also showing up when you indulge in 'should's' - you should do this; I should do that; they should be this way; life should be like this. It shows up when you are judging all that is going on in an inflexible and rigid way; that it 'should' be something else, attempting to place your values and controls on things that are uncontrollable.

Anytime you experience conflict in your relationships or negativity caused by too many or too few people in your life – these are all examples of the dark energy of thunder. You may be too serious, not relaxed and not taking time to enjoy life. Dark collapsed thunder energy also makes you feel intolerant of others who do not share your same drive to work for the greater good and you use this to justify bulldozing over others.

Sometimes dark collapsed thunder energy creates a feeling of abandonment for you. A feeling that the conflict in relationships is caused by people walking away from you, abandoning you in your life.

In some of your relationships, choosing to stay silent becomes thunder inside. It eventually explodes and releases as abrupt, loud chaos.

For some, dark collapsed thunder energy can show up as a belief that you will grow frail and sick and lose your powers, lose your thunder, lose your freedom, as you grow old.

YOUR DAILY PULSE

Intention
In your journal, write this intention for the thunder Daily Pulse:

My intention is to live in the light expanding energy of thunder; to live as a powerful person who brings release and freedom to situations and to others.

Breath prayer
Find a comfortable sitting position, rest your hands in your lap or hold them by your heart. Close your eyes gently, feel your scalp and forehead soften.

Breathe in and breathe out, place your focus and attention on your adrenals (in the middle of your back, on either side of your spine).

Quietly and to yourself, state this affirmation:

"I am inspirational and I am powerful and free and I choose to create safe, strong connections."

Breathe in and breathe out and quietly and to yourself state:

"I reprogram myself towards the light expanding energy of thunder and I breathe in connection and I breathe out disconnection. I breathe in acceptance and I breathe out forcing."

Continue with lovely soft breathing and say a quiet thank you for who you are, exactly as you are.

Journaling

Review the section on the light expanding energy of thunder. All parts of the light expanding energy can be part of your life with intention and conscious deliberate choice. Write today's answers to these questions in your journal.

Q: Where in your life do you feel your power? Power that makes things happen, brings order and structure, creates outcomes?

Q: Light expanding thunder energy is being non-judgmental, broad minded, seeing all perspectives. Is this part of your life?

Q: What healthy connections do you have with others?

Q: How is your thunder energy helping those around you? How does your desire to be of service and help others, show up?

Review the section on the dark collapsed thunder energy and using the technique of third party talk answer the questions below.

Although we have covered all parts of the dark collapsed energy, there are likely only one or two aspects that are showing up in (insert your first name e.g. Brenda's) life right now. Focus on these.

Q: Which part of dark collapsed thunder energy is (Brenda) experiencing now? How does it show up, where and with whom?

Q: What would (Brenda's) life be like if this could turn around and reprogram towards the light expanding energy of thunder?

Write a note to your higher self.

Dear higher self …

This can take the form of a prayer, an asking for help. Asking higher self, your guides, your angels, your god, to create solutions, to intervene on your behalf.

Or it can take more of a meditative form, an asking for wisdom and understanding, for clarity.

It could be a simple thank you to spirit, an exercise in gratitude.

It could also be asking higher self about what your life would be like if you lived in light expanding thunder energy.

Antidote and action

As an antidote to dark collapsed thunder energy and to bring light expanding thunder energy and the profound teachings of the Tao into your life:

> ➢ Connect with others, find ways to be of service
> ➢ Balance your life by getting rid of all of the 'should's' – for yourself and for others
> ➢ Find flow and non-resistance by accepting others and building strong foundations for relationships.

Write down the action you will take to implement this antidote and manifest connection, balance and flow of the thunder trigram.

GEMSTONE

Gemstones are gifts from the earth and carry energy that you can tap into. The gemstone for thunder energy is Jade.

Jade encourages harmonious relationships.

Jade eliminates negativity.

Jade promotes clarity.

ONE CHOICE
OF POSITIVE BEHAVIOUR,
OF LOVING ACTIONS,

HAS AN ENORMOUS IMPACT
ON ALL.

SETH

SUMMARY:

Light expanding thunder energy

Thunder: power and connection; denotes release, heralds nourishment

Intention for Thunder: to live in the light expanding energy of thunder; to live as a powerful person who brings release and freedom to situations and to others.

Affirmation: I am inspirational and I am powerful and free and I choose to create safe, strong connections.

Reprogramming: I reprogram myself towards the light expanding energy of thunder and I breathe in connection and I breathe out disconnection. I breathe in acceptance and I breathe out forcing.

Antidote: Find ways to be of service; remove 'should's' for yourself and others; focus on building strong foundations for relationships.

2.5 YOUR DAILY PULSE
– HEAVEN ENERGY

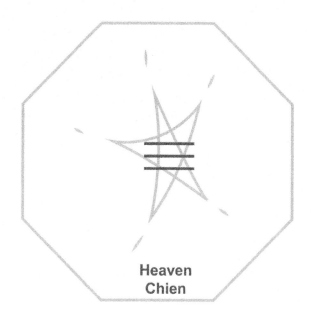

**Heaven
Chien**

UNDERSTANDING OF THE TAO

Through the teachings of the Tao
you deeply appreciate that you are more
than your physical body,
and that you are all connected to each
other.

That when one part is out of balance,
all parts are affected and that life is all
about flow, about non-resistance and
accepting.
Dr. Debra

TRIGRAM OF THE TAO – HEAVEN

When light and expanding, heaven energy represents perspective and support and is creation energy.

When dark and collapsed, heaven energy has no perspective and a limited point of view.

Light expanding heaven energy:

There has never been a concept so dreamed about nor so debated as the concept of heaven. For those who follow Middle Eastern religion (Christianity, Judaism, Islam) heaven is a place. For those who follow eastern philosophy, heaven is a state of being. For some who are simply spiritual, heaven is where they come from, it is home.

Heaven is a mystery, but in all our beliefs around heaven one thing is consistent, heaven is love. It is a positive and loving energy and you may be either coming from there, being there or going there.

In the Tao, heaven represents fundamental creation energy. The trigram of the Tao for heaven is three solid lines, three yang lines. Yang energy is creative, moving, active. This is heaven energy.

Light expanding heaven energy is part of your life on those days when you feel mighty and unrestricted. It is part of your life when you are in an active, doing mode that encourages expansive concepts and new beginnings. It is there when you are both physically active and spiritually connected.

Light expanding heaven energy shows up when you have perspective and understand the importance of both giving and receiving support; when you give help to others and are supported by people who willingly give you a helping hand. Light expanding heaven energy shows up when you are supported by the non-physical world (your God, your guides, your angels) and understand that you are more than your physical body.

You can feel heaven energy within yourself when you are able to have perspective on the meaning of life; when your life has context; when you don't sweat the small stuff.

In the Tao, heaven energy is creation. Creation is one of our deepest yearnings. Your life is a creation.

Dark collapsed heaven energy:

Yet heaven energy can also show up as an inability to put life into perspective. Being unable to give your life context, to see the big picture, to have a broader view point, when your frame of reference is too small with a mostly negative aspect, this is all dark collapsed heaven energy.

The word heaven is emotive and if you don't believe in heaven, feelings of incredulity and skepticism can be very strong. No one can prove whether heaven exists or not, it is a belief that you do or do not have.

Within yourself, dark collapsed heaven energy makes you feel that you don't matter and are rejected. You feel that what you give to others is refused, not accepted, you feel brushed off and dismissed.

In your life, dark collapsed heaven energy shows up as overgeneralizing and expecting bad things to happen, not once, but over and over again. Even in the face of no proof, you wait for the worst to happen.

Dark collapsed heaven energy also makes you focus on a single unpleasant detail in otherwise pleasant events and interactions. You fixate on one small single negative comment or action and have no perspective.

Anytime you have a tendency towards self-pity or indulge in feelings that no one cares, this is dark collapsed heaven energy. When you have the inability to say what you need and when you accept suffering in your life, this is dark collapsed heaven energy. Light expanding heaven energy is the mighty, unrestricted creation of your life, there is no room for self pity.

For some, dark collapsed heaven energy can also show up as feeling helpless before circumstances that you cannot control, misunderstanding that you are indeed the master creator of your life and your experience.

YOUR DAILY PULSE

Intention

In your journal write this intention for the heaven Daily Pulse:

> *My intention is to live in the light expanding energy of heaven; to live as a supported and expanding person who feels mighty and unrestricted.*

Breath prayer

Find a comfortable sitting position, rest your hands in your lap or hold them by your heart. Close your eyes gently, feel your scalp and forehead soften.

Breathe in and breathe out, place your focus and attention on a point six inches (15 cm) above your head.

Quietly and to yourself, state this affirmation:

> *"I am supported and expanding and I choose to feel supported."*

Breathe in and breathe out and quietly and to yourself state:

"I reprogram myself towards the light expanding energy of heaven and I breathe in support and I breathe out rejection. I breathe in unrestricted creation and I breathe out self pity."

Continue with lovely soft breathing and say a quiet thank you for who you are, exactly as you are.

Journaling

Review the section on the light expanding energy of heaven. All parts of the light expanding energy can become part of your life with intention and conscious deliberate choice. Write today's answers to these questions in your journal.

Q: How does the creation energy of heaven show up in your life? Do you ever feel mighty and unrestricted? Where, with whom, when?

Q: Is your life balanced between being physically active and spiritually connected?

Q: Are you good at both giving and receiving support – or is there an imbalance there? What could you do about that?

Q: What is your perspective on the meaning of life?

Review the section on the dark collapsed heaven energy and using the technique of third party talk answer the questions below.

Although we have covered all parts of the dark collapsed energy, there are likely only one or two aspects that are showing up in (insert your first name e.g. Brenda's) life right now. Focus on these.

Q: Which part of dark collapsed heaven energy is (Brenda) experiencing now? How does it show up, where and with whom?

Q: What would (Brenda's) life be like if this could turn around and reprogram towards the light expanding energy of heaven?

Write a note to your higher self.

Dear higher self …

This can take the form of a prayer, an asking for help. Asking higher self, your guides, your angels, your god, to create solutions, to intervene on your behalf.

Or it can take more of a meditative form, an asking for wisdom and understanding, for clarity.

It could be a simple thank you to spirit, an exercise in gratitude.

It could also be asking higher self about what your life would be like if you lived in light expanding heaven energy.

Antidote and action

As an antidote to dark collapsed heaven energy and to bring light expanding heaven energy and the profound teachings of the Tao into your life:

➢ Connect with others by giving support and receiving support.
➢ Balance your life by focusing on a bigger perspective.

> ➤ Find flow and non-resistance by consciously choosing the creation energy of heaven and to feel mighty and unrestricted.

Write down the action that you will take to implement this antidote and manifest connection, balance and flow of the heaven trigram.

GEMSTONE

Gemstones are gifts from the earth and carry energy that you can tap into. The gemstone for heaven energy is Smoky Quartz.

Smoky Quartz links you to the highest realms.

Smoky Quartz improves meditation.

Smoky Quartz brings serenity.

CHOOSE TO BE CONTENT, SATISFIED,
THANKFUL FOR THIS VERY MOMENT.

TRULY THANKFUL; PARTICULARLY IF THE
MOMENT IS UNHAPPY.

IN THIS MOMENT OF UNHAPPINESS YOU
EXPERIENCE AN OPPORTUNITY FOR CHOICE.

WHO WILL YOU BE?

SETH

SUMMARY:

Light expanding heaven energy

Heaven: perspective and support; creation

Intention for Heaven: to live in the light expanding energy of heaven; to live as a supported and expanding person who feels mighty and unrestricted.

Affirmation: I am supported and expanding and I choose to feel supported.

Reprogramming: I reprogram myself towards the light expanding energy of heaven and I breathe in support and I breathe out rejection. I breathe in unrestricted creation and I breathe out self pity.

Antidote: Focus on support - giving and receiving, physical and divine; focus on a bigger perspective; choose the creation energy of heaven, feel mighty and unrestricted.

2.6 YOUR DAILY PULSE
– WATER ENERGY

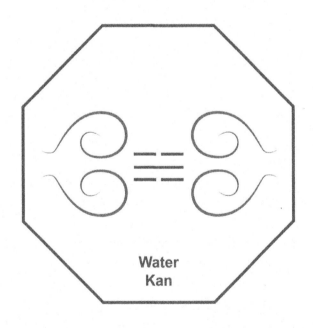

**Water
Kan**

UNDERSTANDING OF THE TAO

Through the teachings
of the Tao
you understand that what is
happening to you,
affects all of us

and that when you are out of balance,
we are all impacted.

Dr. Debra

TRIGRAM OF THE TAO – WATER

When light and expanding, water energy represents flow and empowerment and has depth, is flowing, fluid, reflective and still.

When dark and collapsed, water energy is too much, it overflows, has no boundaries and is destructive.

Light expanding water energy:

I imagine this water energy as the ocean. A huge expanse of water with so much going on beneath the surface. Deep, calm and still. Light expanding water energy has so many layers, as do you. You are as deep as the ocean with as many layers below.

Light expanding water energy is part of your life on those days when you live life in non-resistance; when you focus on a goal and flow downstream.

When you are in the flow of life, your life has purpose and you feel confident, empowered and assured, sharing your journey and your quest for meaning.

Light expanding water energy shows up when you are heart centred and practice compassion toward yourself and others. Light expanding water energy is part of your relationships when you love in a healthy way and create boundaries without enabling and sanctioning others' bad habits and behaviours.

You can feel light expanding water energy within yourself when you choose to feel accepted by others for who you are, exactly as you are.

As the ocean is never full of water, so your heart is never full of love, there is always room for more. The energy of water moves the heart and brings joy to your soul and models the greatest lesson of life – living with flow and non-resistance.

Dark collapsed water energy:
Yet, you also know that water energy can be too much; it overflows and has no boundaries. Water can be completely destructive. It follows the path of least resistance, flowing anywhere and everywhere, spoiling things in its path.

Destructive water energy can be pounding waves, overflowing rivers, rain storms, causing both above ground and underground destruction. In your life, when you are experiencing dark collapsed water energy, you feel overwhelmed. You flow everywhere, you flow nowhere, you also overflow. You become indecisive and focused on unimportant details.

Within yourself, dark collapsed water energy makes you feel that you are not accepted for who you are and you are judged. You expect an unfavourable opinion from others. Those times when you are uncertain and personalize everything, this is the dark energy of water. When you personalize every comment, when every action becomes all about you and others judging you, you are experiencing the dark energy of water.

In your life, dark collapsed water energy is also showing up when you indulge in negative emotional reasoning. Your negative emotions about yourself and others are your gloomy interpretation. Just because you are feeling unhealthy emotions, doesn't mean that they are the truth about a person or situation. Water represents emotions and dark collapsed water energy reflects in your victim mentality and your negative emotional reasoning.

Anytime you feel that you are not living up to expectations or you indulge in constant questioning, which renders you inert and induces procrastination – all examples of the dark energy of water in your life.

Unnecessary worrying – a sign of the dark energy of water.

Dark collapsed water energy can also show up as a belief that only you or your group has the truth and no one else has it.

YOUR DAILY PULSE

Intention

In your journal write this intention for the water Daily Pulse:

> *My intention is to live in the light expanding energy of water; to live as a deep person who flows through life; one who understands non-resistance and lives with quiet reflection.*

Breath prayer

Find a comfortable sitting position, rest your hands in your lap or hold them by your heart. Close your eyes gently, feel your scalp and forehead soften.

Breathe in and breathe out, place your focus and attention on your heart.

Quietly and to yourself, state:

> *"I am compassionate and I am confident and deep and I choose to feel accepted."*

Breathe in and breathe out and quietly and to yourself state:

> *"I reprogram myself towards the light expanding energy of water and I breathe in being decisive and I breathe out indecision. I breathe in assurance and I breathe out uncertainty."*

Continue with lovely soft breathing and say a quiet thank you for who you are, exactly as you are.

Journaling

Review the section on the light expanding energy of water. All parts of the light expanding energy can become part of your life with intention and conscious deliberate choice. Write today's answers to these questions in your journal.

Q: Do you know what it feels like to focus on a goal and flow downstream? What happens when you do? How can you bring more of that into your life now?

Q: Do you ever feel confident and assured? When you feel so good that you share your journey and quest for meaning in life.

Q: Would you define your relationships as healthy, with boundaries?

Q: What does a life of flow and non-resistance feel like? Why can't you have more of that?

Review the section on the dark collapsed water energy and using the technique of third party talk answer the questions below.

Although we have covered all parts of the dark collapsed energy, there are likely only one or two aspects that are showing up in (insert your first name e.g. Brenda's) life right now. Focus on these.

Q: Which part of dark collapsed water energy is (Brenda) experiencing now? How does it show up, where and with whom?

Q: What would (Brenda's) life be like if this could turn around and reprogram towards the light expanding energy of water?

Write a note to your higher self.

Dear higher self …

This can take the form of a prayer, an asking for help. Asking higher self, your guides, your angels, your god, to create solutions, to intervene on your behalf.

Or it can take more of a meditative form, an asking for wisdom and understanding, for clarity.

It could be a simple thank you to spirit, an exercise in gratitude.

It could also be asking higher self about what your life would be like if you lived in light expanding water energy.

Antidote and action

As an antidote to dark collapsed water energy and to bring light expanding water energy and the profound teachings of the Tao into your life:

➢ Connect with others, to create healthy boundaries.
➢ Balance your life by choosing to feel accepted.
➢ Find flow and non-resistance by focusing on a goal, taking the next best step and flowing downstream.

Write down the action you will take to implement this anti-dote and manifest connection, balance and flow of the water trigram.

GEMSTONE

Gemstones are gifts from the earth and carry energy that you can tap into. The gemstone for water energy is Onyx.

Onyx increases personal power.

Onyx builds vitality and assists with inner strength.

Onyx helps with trusting your heart.

MOMENT BY MOMENT, AN ASKING

'WHAT IS MY NEXT BEST STEP',

THIS IS THE PATH TO JOY.

SETH

SUMMARY:

Light expanding water energy

Water: flow and empowerment; depth, flowing, fluid, reflective, still

Intention for Water: to live in the light expanding energy of water; to live as a deep person who flows through life; one who understands non-resistance and lives with quiet reflection.

Affirmation: I am compassionate and I am confident and deep and I choose to feel accepted.

Reprogramming: I reprogram myself towards the light expanding energy of water and I breathe in being decisive and I breathe out indecision. I breathe in assurance and I breathe out uncertainty.

Antidote: Create healthy boundaries; choose to feel accepted; focus on a goal and flowing downstream.

2.7 YOUR DAILY PULSE
- MOUNTAIN ENERGY

Mountain
Ken

UNDERSTANDING OF THE TAO

*As you accept your soul's plan
for this lifetime, your soul's desire
for a life experience -*

*you also understand that
this planet that you live on
is a creative environment
and that with your free will
you are creating your life.*

Dr. Debra

TRIGRAM OF THE TAO – MOUNTAIN

When light and expanding, mountain energy represents trust and wisdom and is constant, everlasting, durable, all seeing, always there.

When dark and collapsed, mountain energy is rigid and stuck.

Light expanding mountain energy:

Mountains are incredible! I remember speaking with a young girl who was born and raised on the flat Canadian prairies, as she described her first experience of mountains. The awe and wonder that she felt as she drove through the Canadian Rocky Mountains. Knowing that they had always been there. The miracle of their height and her imagining of what you could see from the top of a mountain. The courage that she felt was needed to climb a mountain; the many paths, the many different ways to get to the top.

She understood that mountains were not to be conquered, but they provided opportunities for us to know ourselves.

Light expanding mountain energy is part of your life on those days when you tap into your innate wisdom and you feel connected to spirit and your higher self.

Light expanding mountain energy is about having faith in life; conviction and confidence that things will work out for the best. Faith is a choice to trust in life and to trust your strength and your wisdom. Faith is trusting in your beliefs, your God, the world and living with strength, wisdom and steadiness; feeling peaceful and full of hope.

You can sense light expanding mountain energy within yourself when you push the boundaries of beliefs and share your beliefs with others. Light expanding mountain energy helps you be a great communicator, allowing you to make difficult and intangible ideas easy to understand.

Mountains are impressive. Mountains are firmly grounded on earth and reach up to the heavens; they are deeply connected to both physical and spiritual.

Dark collapsed mountain energy:

Yet, you can also imagine that dark collapsed mountain energy is rigid and stuck. Mountains don't move. Dark collapsed mountain energy causes beliefs and attitudes that are uncompromising and inflexible.

Mountains are huge, you can't ignore them. They throw immense shadows. Dark collapsed mountain energy often manifests as having a superior attitude; those times when you are cold and aloof and impatient with others.

Within yourself, dark collapsed mountain energy makes you feel that people are out to get you and you will be betrayed. You feel they will turn on you and be disloyal and violate your confidence.

In your life, dark collapsed mountain energy causes you to feel that life isn't fair; that things never work out in your favour. No matter what you do, it just isn't fair.

You may question the point of life. You may wonder at the meaning of life. You may lack faith and not trust the process of life. You may indulge in doubt and constant questioning.

Dark collapsed mountain energy also encourages polarized thinking; a way of looking at the world that is black and white. No compromise. No concessions. No understanding of another's point of view or life experience. No tolerance.

Dark collapsed mountain energy can show up as a belief that people are basically bad. As a human race we are defective. There's no one you can trust, there is nothing to have faith in.

YOUR DAILY PULSE

Intention
In your journal write this intention for the mountain Daily Pulse:

My intention is to live in the light expanding energy of mountain; to live as a strong, steady and wise person who has faith and chooses to trust life.

Breath prayer

Find a comfortable sitting position, rest your hands in your lap or hold them by your heart. Close your eyes gently, feel your scalp and forehead soften.

Breathe in and breathe out, place your focus and attention on your third eye, that space between your eyebrows on your lower forehead.

Quietly and to yourself, state this affirmation:

"I am spiritual and I am strong, steady and wise and I choose to relax and trust."

Breathe in and breathe out and quietly and to yourself state:

"I reprogram myself towards the light expanding energy of mountain and I breathe in trust and I breathe out distrust. I breathe in hope and I breathe out doubt."

Continue with lovely soft breathing and say a quiet thank you for who you are, exactly as you are.

Journaling

Review the section on the light expanding energy of mountain. All parts of the light expanding energy can become part of your life with intention and conscious deliberate choice. Write today's answers to these questions in your journal.

Q: What does it feel like to be connected to your innate wisdom?

Q: What would a life based on faith and trust be like?

Q: Are you taking the time to explore beliefs and intangibles and then share them with others?

Q: Mountain energy is firmly rooted to earth and reaches up to the heavens. What does this mean for you in your life?

Review the section on the dark collapsed mountain energy and using the technique of third party talk answer the questions below.

Although we have covered all parts of the dark collapsed energy, there are likely only one or two aspects that are showing up in (insert your first name e.g. Brenda's) life right now. Focus on these.

Q: Which part of dark collapsed mountain energy is (Brenda) experiencing now? How does it show up, where and with whom?

Q: What would (Brenda's) life be like if this could turn around and reprogram towards the light expanding energy of mountain?

Write a note to your higher self.

Dear higher self ...

This can take the form of a prayer, an asking for help. Asking higher self, your guides, your angels, your god, to create solutions, to intervene on your behalf.

Or it can take more of a meditative form, an asking for wisdom and understanding, for clarity.

It could be a simple thank you to spirit, an exercise in gratitude.

It could also be asking higher self about what your life would be like if you lived in light expanding mountain energy.

Antidote and action

As an antidote to dark collapsed mountain energy and to bring light expanding mountain energy and the profound teachings of the Tao into your life:

> ➢ Connect with others by 'walking in their shoes'.
> ➢ Balance your life by focusing on your spiritual connection and being constant, certain and strong.
> ➢ Find flow and non-resistance by consciously choosing to have faith and trust the flow of life.

Write down the action you will take to implement this antidote for connection, balance and flow of the mountain trigram.

GEMSTONE

Gemstones are gifts from the earth and carry energy that you can tap into. The gemstone for mountain energy is Lapis Lazuli.

Lapis Lazuli assists with accessing universal knowledge.

Lapis Lazuli promotes connection.

STAY QUIET, STAY STILL, STAY
PEACEFUL, ESCAPE,

THIS IS OFTEN HOW TO CREATE THE
BEST RESOLUTION.

IN AN ENERGETIC PAUSE, YOU SEE SO
MUCH BIRTH
AS EVENTS ARE ALIGNED.

SETH

SUMMARY:

Light expanding mountain energy

Mountain: trust and wisdom; constancy, everlasting, durable, all seeing, always there

Intention for Mountain: to live in the light expanding energy of mountain; to live as a strong, steady and wise person who has faith and chooses to trust life.

Affirmation: I am spiritual and I am strong, steady and wise and I choose to relax and trust.

Reprogramming: I reprogram myself towards the light expanding energy of mountain and I breathe in trust and I breathe out distrust. I breathe in hope and I breathe out doubt.

Antidote: Choose to walk in another's shoes; work on spiritual connection; focus on faith and trusting.

2.8   YOUR DAILY PULSE
- WIND ENERGY

Wind
Sun

UNDERSTANDING OF THE TAO

*The object of spiritual practice
is to become
'one with the Tao',*

*to synchronize
with the pulse of nature,*

*to allow and experience
non-resistance.*
Dr. Debra

TRIGRAM OF THE TAO – WIND

When light and expanding, wind energy represents kindness and generosity and is always moving and gentle.

When dark and collapsed, wind energy is strong, unsettling and destructive.

Light expanding wind energy:

Wind is so curious to me. It's invisible. You can only see, hear or feel its effect. You can see the rustling of the leaves as a gentle breeze blows through a forest. A breeze turns wind chimes into a song. You can feel it on your skin as it cools you down on a hot summer day. But in and of itself, wind is invisible – yet the effect of wind is profound. Wind is like the positive emotions of love and kindness, which can't be seen, but certainly can be felt.

Light expanding wind energy is part of your life on those days when you feel generous and kind and enjoy sharing your abundance of joy, love and money with others.

Light expanding wind energy shows up when you are providing direction to make things better; when you are using your inner power and energy to make life better. It is also there when you feel like a supercharged individual who easily commands others and uses strong personal chi and power for the benefit of all.

You can sense light expanding wind energy within yourself when you are thinking clearly. Light expanding wind energy is always moving and creating change, making decisions and making things happen.

A gentle wind is cleansing. A gentle wind is cooling. A gentle wind can blow all your cares away. A gentle wind is angel's breath.

Dark collapsed wind energy:

Yet, you also know that wind energy can also be too strong, unsettling and destructive. Negative emotions have been described as the wind that blows out the lamp of the mind. When life gets difficult, its important to remind yourself to bend with the wind to remain unbroken.

The words gale-force wind, hurricane and typhoon bring up images of destruction and devastation. In your life, when you are experiencing dark collapsed wind energy, you are always impacting others in a destructive way, leaving wreckage in your wake.

Dark collapsed wind energy makes you too determined and you find it hard to see how others are affected by your actions, which can be unkind and abusive.

Within yourself, dark collapsed wind energy makes you feel that they are out to get you and you feel exploited. Those times when you feel selfishly taken advantage of by others – you are experiencing the dark energy of wind.

In your life, dark collapsed wind energy is also showing up when you create control fallacies - feeling helpless under external controls. These are usually a direct result of your misinterpretation of events and of life; a real manifestation of dark collapsed wind energy.

Anytime you blame others for your life situation. Anytime you don't take responsibility for your life – all further examples of the dark energy of wind.

Blaming others is also part of your control fallacy, as you find it easier to feel helpless under external controls and blame others, than to take control of your own life.

Feelings of scarcity. An inability to accept happiness for yourself or for others. Withholding your love and restricting yourself. Worrying that life as you know it will be taken away – the dark collapsed energy of wind.

Dark collapsed wind energy can show up as a belief that your body is inferior; that your flesh is inherently weak and its appetites are wrong.

YOUR DAILY PULSE

Intention
In your journal write this intention for the wind Daily Pulse:

My intention is to live in the light expanding energy of wind; to live as a kind, gentle, curious and connected person who uses inner power and energy to make life better.

Breath prayer

Find a comfortable sitting position, rest your hands in your lap or hold them by your heart. Close your eyes gently, feel your scalp and forehead soften.

Breathe in and breathe out, place your focus and attention on your pineal gland, which is shaped like a tiny pinecone in the middle of your brain. In the middle from front to back and left to right.

Quietly and to yourself, state this affirmation:

"I am intellectual and I am curious and connected and I choose to be kind."

Breathe in and breathe out and quietly and to yourself state:

"I reprogram myself towards the light expanding energy of wind and I breathe in generosity and I breathe out withholding. I breathe in kindness and I breathe out restriction".

Continue with lovely soft breathing and say a quiet thank you for who you are, exactly as you are.

Journaling

Review the section on the light expanding energy of wind. All parts of the light expanding energy can become part of your life with intention and conscious, deliberate choice. Write today's answers to these questions in your journal.

Q: What happens in your life when you are generous and share your blessings?

Q: Do you feel your inner power and energy? How do you use it?

Q: When do you feel supercharged with strong personal chi? With whom? Why is that?

Q: Wind creates change. It is cleansing and cooling. Do you see those characteristics in your life?

Review the section on the dark collapsed wind energy and using the technique of third party talk answer the questions below.

Although we have covered all parts of the dark collapsed energy, there are likely only one or two aspects that are showing up in (insert your first name e.g. Brenda's) life right now. Focus on these.

Q: Which part of dark collapsed wind energy is (Brenda) experiencing now? How does it show up, where and with whom?

Q: What would (Brenda's) life be like if this could turn around and reprogram towards the light expanding energy of wind?

Write a note to your higher self.

Dear higher self …

This can take the form of a prayer, an asking for help. Asking higher self, your guides, your angels, your god, to create solutions, to intervene on your behalf.

Or it can take more of a meditative form, an asking for wisdom and understanding, for clarity.

It could be a simple thank you to spirit, an exercise in gratitude.

It could also be asking higher self about what your life would be like if you lived in light expanding wind energy.

Antidote and action

As an antidote to dark collapsed wind energy and to bring light expanding wind energy and the profound teachings of the Tao into your life, follow these key understandings:

➤ Connect with others by sharing and being kind.
➤ Balance your life by focusing on your curiosity and connection.
➤ Find flow and non-resistance by consciously including and accepting others. By sharing your blessings.

Write down the action you will take to implement this antidote for connection, balance and flow of the wind trigram.

GEMSTONE

Gemstones are gifts from the earth and carry energy that you can tap into. The gemstone for wind energy is Amethyst

Amethyst brings good fortune.

Amethyst clears personal energy.

Amethyst promotes clear thinking and respect.

STAY IN YOUR LIGHT,
ALL IS WELL,

LET GENTLENESS
AND KINDNESS VIBRATE
TOWARDS YOU.

SETH

SUMMARY:

Light expanding wind energy

Wind: kindness and generosity; always moving and gentle

Intention for Wind: to live in the light expanding energy of wind to live as a kind, gentle, curious and connected person who uses their inner power and energy to make life better.

Affirmation: I am intellectual and I am curious and connected and I choose to be kind.

Reprogramming: I reprogram myself towards the light expanding energy of wind and I breathe in generosity and I breathe out withholding. I breathe in kindness and I breathe out restriction.

Antidote: Focus on sharing and being kind; focus on curiosity and connection; consciously include and accept others.

2.9   YOUR DAILY PULSE
– TAI CHI ENERGY

UNDERSTANDING OF THE TAO

The Tao is accepting that you are
only here on earth for one reason -

the evolution of your soul -
and this is accomplished through
experiencing negative collapsed energy

and choosing positive expanding energy.

Dr. Debra

EIGHT TRIGRAMS OF THE TAO FORM
THE YIN YANG, TAI CHI

When light and expanding, tai chi energy is balanced, allowing and non-resistant.

When dark and collapsed, tai chi energy is unbalanced.

Light expanding Tai Chi energy:

The tai chi is a composite of all the eight trigrams of the Tao and represents balance. Balance is defined as mental steadiness or emotional stability; a habit of calm behaviour and judgment. Synonyms for balance include poise and composure. Balance is harmony, tranquility and peace.

In life, the tai chi is seen as a balance between being and doing; between holding on and letting go.

Balance is not outside of you, not something that you find. Balance is a state of being within you, that you create.

The way to create balance in your life is through your state of mind - your mental steadiness and the way you feel - your emotional stability. Balance is not found through managing the external factors in your life. It is not through time management of what you do for work and what you do for family, and what you do for others. Balance is created internally.

Light expanding tai chi energy creates inner calm. It is being allowing of others and non-resistant. It fosters confidence, trust and hope. Light expanding tai chi energy helps you live with acceptance, full of inner certainty and balance.

You can sense light expanding tai chi energy within yourself when your life is moving forward. It is with you when you are helping others move forward in their lives by being a trusted advisor who provides valuable guidance and great advice. With expanding tai chi energy you are able to give perspective and understanding about life and you experience great joy from helping others.

In the Tao, the eight trigrams combine together to form a perfect balance of active yang doing and passive yin being. This is tai chi energy.

Dark collapsed Tai Chi energy:
Yet, tai chi energy can also show up as living an unbalanced life. The biggest obstacle to living with harmony, tranquility and peace

is looking for balance outside of you; blaming outside pressures for your lack of poise and composure.

A consequence of living an unbalanced life, of giving in to dark collapsed tai chi energy, is that you feel that you are not accepted for what you do. You feel criticized and because of this you find fault with others and feel that others find fault with you.

In your life, dark collapsed tai chi shows up as a control fallacy that says that 'I am so important, I can control everything'. Dark tai chi energy is not understanding the balance between what you can control and what you cannot control.

Within yourself, dark collapsed tai chi energy is always needing to be right, proving that your opinions and actions are right. You become confrontational and dictatorial, telling others what to do rather than guiding them to their own decisions.

Dark collapsed tai chi energy can also show up as a belief that life is a valley of sorrows.

Yin yang, tai chi energy is represented by a symbol that shows perfect balance, where the light is balanced by the dark and the dark is balanced by the light. In life, happiness would lose its meaning if it were not balanced by sadness. Love would not be recognized if it were not balanced by fear.

YOUR DAILY PULSE

Intention
In your journal write this intention for the tai chi Daily Pulse:

My intention is to live in the light expanding energy of the tai chi; to live a life that is balanced, flowing, peaceful and tranquil.

Breath prayer

Find a comfortable sitting position, rest your hands in your lap or hold them by your heart. Close your eyes gently, feel your scalp and forehead soften.

Breathe in and breathe out, place your focus and attention on your navel, the mid point, the balance point of your body.

Quietly and to yourself, state this affirmation:

"I know my life's plan, I am happy and whole and I choose to be allowing."

Breathe in and breathe out and quietly and to yourself state:

"I reprogram myself towards the light expanding energy of the tai chi and I breathe in allowing and I breathe out resistance. I breathe in flow and I breathe out struggle."

Continue with lovely soft breathing and say a quiet thank you for who you are, exactly as you are.

Journaling

Review the section on the light expanding energy of the tai chi. All parts of the light expanding energy can become part of your life with intention and conscious deliberate choice. Write today's answers to these questions in your journal.

Q: What does the perspective that balance is created internally mean to you and your life?

Q: If balance is a state of being, what could you do differently?

Q: How can you find your inner calm? What are you doing to move your life forward?

Q: Rhythm and ritual create balance, how can you make your Daily Pulse a part of your life going forward?

Review the section on the dark collapsed tai chi energy and using the technique of third party talk answer the questions below.

Although we have covered all parts of the dark collapsed energy, there are likely only one or two aspects that are showing up in (insert your first name e.g. Brenda's) life right now. Focus on these.

Q: Which part of dark collapsed tai chi energy is (Brenda) experiencing now? How does it show up, where and with whom?

Q: What would (Brenda's) life be like if this could turn around and reprogram towards the light expanding energy of tai chi?

Write a note to your higher self.

Dear higher self ...

This can take the form of a prayer, an asking for help. Asking higher self, your guides, your angels, your god, to create solutions, to intervene on your behalf.

Or it can take more of a meditative form, an asking for wisdom and understanding, for clarity.

It could be a simple thank you to spirit, an exercise in gratitude.

It could also be asking higher self about what your life would be like if you lived in light expanding tai chi energy.

Antidote and action

As an antidote to dark collapsed tai chi energy and to bring light expanding tai chi energy and the profound teachings of the Tao into your life, follow these key understandings:

> ➢ Connect with others by allowing them to be who they are and have their own life experience.
> ➢ Balance your life by focusing on living with harmony and emotional steadiness.
> ➢ Find flow and non-resistance by consciously choosing to introduce rhythm and ritual into your life. Create a daily habit of pulse, sanctuary and connection.

Write down the action you will take to implement this antidote and manifest connection, balance and flow of the tai chi.

GEMSTONE

Gemstones are gifts from the earth and carry energy that we can tap into. The gemstone for tai chi energy is Citrine.

Citrine balances and heals.

Citrine brings the energy of the sun into life.

THERE IS SOME THOUGHT THAT
GOOD DEEDS ARE BIG DEEDS
AND THAT IS TOO MUCH FOR
AN INDIVIDUAL TO UNDERTAKE.

BUT ANY POSITIVE ENERGY,
DIRECTED IN ANY WAY

IS FUNDAMENTALLY IMPORTANT
TO THE PLANET.
SETH

SUMMARY:

Light expanding Tai Chi energy

Tai Chi: balance; allowing, non-resistant

Intention for Tai Chi: to live in the light expanding energy of the tai chi; to live a life that is balanced, flowing, peaceful and tranquil.

Affirmation: I know my life's plan, I am happy and whole and I choose to be allowing.

Reprogramming: I reprogram myself towards the light expanding energy of the tai chi and I breathe in allowing and I breathe out resistance. I breathe in flow and I breathe out struggle.

Antidote: Allow others their own life experience; focus on living with balance and emotional steadiness; introduce rhythm and ritual into your life – your Daily Pulse.

Section 3

sharing the daily pulse with others

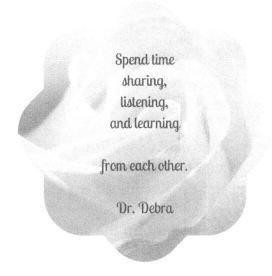

Spend time
sharing,
listening,
and learning

from each other.

Dr. Debra

SHARING THE DAILY PULSE EXPERIENCE IN A GROUP

In the process of creating the Daily Pulse for Brenda, I shared these teachings with others, in both private one-on-one settings as well as with groups.

The Daily Pulse is a profound transformational tool whether you use the guidance alone or share it with others who are also coping with life's challenges and wanting to be happier.

A guide to hosting a Daily Pulse group:

The purpose of a Daily Pulse gathering is not to solve one individual's problems but rather to spend time sharing, listening and learning from each others' experiences.

Focus on one of the trigrams of the Tao at a time. Encourage participants to work through the lesson individually, ahead of time and then come together to discuss their experience and understandings.

Our philosophy for group gatherings is to provide a forum for thoughts and ideas to be expressed and explored. It's important to ensure each person feels comfortable in the group and leaves the interaction feeling heard.

The process requires a group host to guide the conversation and could include meditation, yoga or qi gong (or other metaphysical activity) at the beginning and end of the time together.

Active engagement for the group host:

Here are some tips for positive group facilitation.

Relax: Each group is different, with its own energy. Each individual's understandings are different too. The Daily Pulse will stimulate each person to find their own understanding and insights.

It is not about you, you don't need to have all the answers. Your work is guiding others through the Daily Pulse and providing space for a spiritual conversation.

There are no right or wrong understandings; let the work stimulate each individual's unique experience.

Get everyone engaged. Be sensitive to someone holding the floor and dominating the conversation or to someone who is having difficulty finding their voice.

Let participants in the group feel that what they are going to say is important. Don't interrupt, and be aware if someone is being talked over.

Don't make assumptions by finishing sentences, you may miss the magic of the real learning experience.

Don't feel the need to fill the silence and the pauses; sometimes it takes time to formulate thoughts and express them.

Releases: In conversations like these, sometimes a participant will need a deep release, a good cry. Let them release in respectful silence. Don't feel the need to make it 'all better'. Crying is the therapy.

Never touch during a crying release as this distraction generally stops it flowing. If hugs are appropriate, wait for a better time, such as during a break.

To guide the conversation:

At each gathering at the SolePath Institute, to set the tone for group interaction, we welcome everyone and then start by reading aloud our Code of Conduct. You may use this one or create one of your own.

The SolePath community code for participants is to be present in expanding energy, participate in my LightPaths, to be my best. To participate, fully determined to be 'all in'. To show respect to all present, to treat others as I would like to be treated. To walk the talk, to always ensure that my words and actions are a match. To leave all distractions at the door.

The SolePath community pledge is to honour the gifts and greatness of all present. To see all in the gathering as perfect eternal souls having an earth experience and doing the best that they can. To honour the shared purpose and intention of the gathering. Because who knows what we can accomplish together, for us all.

Intention
Begin the group session by reading the intention for the trigram of the Tao that you will be working on together.

Breath Prayer
Experience the Daily Pulse breath prayer together.

As the host, read the breath prayer, affirmation and reprogramming transformation out loud while participants sit with their eyes closed or lie on a mat.

Trigram
Read aloud the section on the light and dark of the trigram that you are working on together. If the group is intimate enough, go around the room and give each person an opportunity to share their experience and understandings when they worked through the trigram on their own.

The following questions are suggestions to stimulate the conversation:

Q: What is your experience of the light of the trigram? How can you bring more into your life? What choices do you have to live the light of the trigram?

Q: What is your experience of the dark of the trigram? How can you leave that behind? What's keeping you in the dark of the trigram, what's keeping you stuck?

Q: What were your understandings as you completed the journaling, what insights did you receive? For the light and for the dark?

Q: What action did you take for the antidote and what was the effect of that? For you and for others?

Q: What was your experience of the gemstone, how did the energy of the gemstone affect your understanding of the trigram of the Tao? How did you use the gemstone throughout your day?

A Daily Pulse gathering will usually take ninety minutes, depending on the size of the group.

At the SolePath Institute, we enjoy tea together and encourage participants to bring a treat for sharing. There is something really unifying about enjoying food together and if you find the topic is particularly intense for participants, a snack break allows time for the teachings to be absorbed and processed.

APPENDIX I – BRENDA'S JOURNAL

With Brenda's permission, here is a copy of her journal showing her understandings and insights as she moved through the teachings of the Daily Pulse.

Brenda's journal is an example of her learning, challenges and growth as she moved through the connection, balance and flow of each trigram of the Tao.

Your journaling may be similar, or it may be completely different depending on what your soul needs. Brenda's journal is here as one example and to stimulate your own ideas.

Dear Reader,

I hope that my journal will be of some assistance to you. I worked on this over many weeks, completing Daily Pulse trigrams each and every day. Sometimes a trigram would really flow for me and I would complete it in one or two days, sometimes I had to reach deeper to find the gift of the lesson and these trigrams could take more than a week to get through.

I found it really helpful to schedule a regular time of day to do this work. This helped me regain some rhythm in my life and it was very healing to see that I was able to create moments of light despite what was going on in my life.

I was amazed that as I moved through each Daily Pulse trigram that my thoughts and reflections went much deeper than my daily cares and fears. It was a surprisingly beautiful distraction and a meditative experience.

I'm going to work my way through all of the trigrams of the Daily Pulse again and am looking forward to seeing the difference and growth in my journaling.

I feel really privileged to know that sharing my journey is part of your healing. Life can be hard, but I feel really hopeful again.

Love, Brenda

Fire Trigram

Intention:
My intention is to live in the light expanding energy of fire; to live as a clear, warm, bright and enlightened person who has courage and leads by example.

Affirmation:
I am charismatic and I am bright and aware and I choose to be true to myself. I reprogram myself towards the light expanding energy of fire and I breathe in growth and I breathe out fear. I breathe in courage and I breathe out feeling small.

Light expanding fire energy:
Q: What happens in life when you allow yourself to shine, when you feel bright and aware?

A: It's been so long since I allowed myself to shine. I used to notice people looking at me in public places, drawn to my brightness. But now I feel that not only do I feel dark, I even look dark. To myself for sure, and to others too. When I feel bright, I look bright and I know that the world is a good place.

Q: What does your journey of personal growth and self-development look like?

A: My journey of personal growth has stalled.

I've been so focused on what's wrong in my life – the health of my loved ones and the fear around losing my job. Personal growth seems so far away from me. I'd love to get it going again. Is this possible? Maybe I could start with reading a new spiritual author.

Q: Do you have courage? Courage to be yourself, courage to be independent, courage to walk your own path?

A: I usually do have courage! All my life I've had courage. I'm just not sure why I feel so weak now. Yes, illness is scary and so is wondering where the money will come from – but I don't think I've ever given in to the weakness like this before. I am courageous – usually.

Q: How do you interact with others? Are the words - open-minded, enlightened, approachable, responsive, thoughtful - part of your interactions?

A: I used to look forward to interactions with others, now I feel closed off. Maybe its just time to fake it till I make it? I could start today – being more open and bright with others.

Dark collapsed fire energy:
Note to myself – remember to use the third person talk to help me get a bit more objectivity.

Q: Which part of the dark fire energy is Brenda experiencing now:

A: Brenda is experiencing "feel the world is a dangerous place and feeling afraid". This is about Brenda losing her job.

A: Brenda is also experiencing "jumping to negative conclusions". This is about the ill health of her loved ones.

Q: What would life be like if Brenda could turn this around and reprogram towards the light expanding energy of fire?

A: If Brenda could bring her focus to the 'now' she would be happier. As Brenda looks at the things that are causing her to be afraid and feel so small – she can also see that each day that she makes it through is a victory. Not all days are so bad. Although her worries are always rolling around her brain – she is able to cope better some days. That's a victory.

I DO HAVE COURAGE! I AM COURAGEOUS!

Dear Higher Self

I am asking for help. I am asking to remember that I am a courageous person. I know that I sometimes forget. I am asking my angels and my guides to intervene, to show me the love and beauty in my life. to help me be a light and bright person just like the energy of fire.

Antidote and Action:

1. *Connect with others by sharing your light.*
   I will make a real effort to make someone I encounter feel good.
2. *Balance your life by focusing on your personal growth and individual development. I will find a new spiritual book to read.*
3. *Find flow, non-resistance by consciously not making assumptions about what others are doing, thinking or feeling. Let them be.*
   I will be cautious around what I am thinking and feeling and consciously choose not to make assumptions.
4. *I will carry tigers eye with me in my purse to help me feel more sparkly and alive.*

<u>Earth trigram</u>

Intention:
My intention is to live in the light expanding energy of earth; to live as a nourishing and nourished person who keeps a sense of self in relationships.

Affirmation:
I know who I am, I am important and significant and I choose to feel valued. I reprogram myself towards the light expanding energy of earth and I breathe in worthiness and I breathe out unworthiness. I breathe in nourishment and I breathe out sacrifice.

Light expanding earth energy:
Q: Is it as easy for you to nourish yourself, as it is to nourish others?

A: I feel that I have lost myself in my worry and anxiety around my loved ones and my work situation. Nourishing myself? Not only have I forgotten how to do that, but I've forgotten that's its even important.

Q: What might change in your life if you did put on your oxygen mask first'?

A: I can't really see how to put on my oxygen mask first. I can't really see that yet. There's a part of me that feels that this is selfish behaviour.

As I write this, I know that if I don't take care of myself it will only add to the burden of the situation if I get mentally or physically sick. Perhaps fear can be a motivation to look after myself?

Q: How would your life feel if you did give and receive love easily, effortlessly connect with others and feel a deep sense of belonging?

A: I do give and receive love easily – with my inner circle. I do connect effortlessly – with my inner circle.

I do feel a deep sense of belonging – with my inner circle. Perhaps it's time to expand my inner circle and create new meaningful relationships?

Do I have the energy for that? Not yet. But maybe with this new awareness, I will attract what I need to me?

Q: What could you allow into your life to experience more light expanding energy of earth – for yourself and for others?

A: Be nourished and be nourishing. What if I focused my thoughts and energy on this idea, rather than on worry and anxiety? Could I do that?

Dark collapsed earth energy:
Note to myself – remember to use the third person talk to help me get a bit more objectivity.

Q: Which part of the dark earth energy is Brenda experiencing now:

A: Brenda is experiencing "absorbing too much" and "feeling help-less". Wow, that feels heavy!

Q: What would life be like if Brenda could turn this around and reprogram towards the light expanding energy of earth?

A: Brenda just needs to be reminded of the big picture of life. Reminded that life is all about 'stuff' that happens, things that she has no control over, things that create hurt and anxiety. That's life. Brenda also needs to remember that her guides have promised her that she is safe, that all is well and that there isn't anything she can't cope with. That's life. (Can I do this?)

Dear Higher Self

I am asking for wisdom and understanding. For the peace that comes from understanding that my life is more than just my day to day worries. That my life is also about my soul evolution and that I am truly safe. I need to remember that you stand by my side and that we are in this life together.

Antidote and Action:

1. Connect with others by allowing them to nourish you and nourishing them.

I will keep an awareness of the balance between being nourished and also nourishing others.

2. Balance your life by focusing on your self love and who you are.

   I will keep my life in perspective and remember that I am a spiritual being having an earth incarnation. There is nothing happening in my life that I cannot cope with.

3. Find flow, non-resistance by consciously choosing not to be so hard on yourself; and making a choice not to be over sensitive to perceived criticism.

   I will stop being so critical of myself, as I struggle to get out of my dark energy. I will give myself credit for the personal nourishing work that I am doing.

4. I will carry rose quartz with me in my purse to help me find peace and emotional healing.

Lake trigram

Intention:
My intention is to live in the light expanding energy of lake; to live as a positive, full and fun person who is creative and full of ideas and imagination.

Affirmation:
I am intuitive and I am fun and full and I choose to have fun. I reprogram myself towards the light expanding energy of lake and I breathe in positivity and I breathe out pessimism. I breathe in happiness and I breathe out negativity.

Light expanding lake energy:
Q: What does a 'glass half full' life look like to you?

A: Wow – I don't even know anymore! I need to get back there, to 'glass half full'. When I was younger I had a deep knowing that life would work out and it's what helped me have a positive attitude to life. When things were tough I knew that I just had to get through them and life would be good on the other side. This time with losing my job and the ill health in my family I seem to have lost my optimism. A glass half full life looks like a life that absorbs the punches because deep inside you know that life will be good to you.

Q: If you could find a more positive frame of mind, what could be possible?

A: It would just make life more tolerable. It would just make the tough times easier to bear. I used to be this way. I wonder what happened?

Q: How do you engage in life? Are you playful and fun? Creative and expressive? Do you bring happiness to yourself and those around you?

A: I've definitely got too serious. It almost seems wrong to be wanting to have playfulness and fun in my life. It seems frivolous. Yet, I miss having fun. I've also let my creative hobbies fall away. I used to paint and draw but haven't for a long time. I just haven't felt inspired and also haven't felt that I had the time. I always feel better when I'm being creative and what could be wrong with making time to paint?

Q: How could better communication make your life easier and happier?

A: I do keep it all inside. All of my fear and worry. I know that a burden shared is a burden halved but I don't want to bother others with my anxieties. I also sometimes feel that to talk about my fears makes them all the more real. So I keep it all inside. I know that this isn't healthy for me and even writing this down I realize that I need to find a way to communicate what is going on inside of me.

Dark collapsed lake energy:
Note to myself – remember to use the third person talk to help me get a bit more objectivity.

Q: Which part of the dark lake energy is Brenda experiencing now:

A: Brenda is experiencing "dwell on the dark and filter out the positive". This is about Brenda's family ill health. And "closed to the flow of possibilities". This is about Brenda losing her job.

Q: What would life be like if Brenda could turn this around and reprogram towards the light expanding energy of lake?

A: Brenda used to feel that when one door closed another would open. So losing a job was never a big deal because there was another better one waiting around the corner. Brenda didn't just play lip service to that, she really and truly believed that.

Where has that gone! To remember that positive, upbeat person for whom life always worked out would be a blessing.

Dear Higher Self

I truly am a positive person, I just can't seem to find her anymore. Please help me to rediscover my optimistic side.

Thank you for reminding me that life does work out, please show me the way back to the peace of that knowing.

Antidote and Action:

1. Connect with others by making time for fun together.
   I will organize a playful and fun activity with my family. No agenda – only fun, together.
2. Balance your life by focusing on clear, honest direct communication.
   I will find a way to let others know how I am feeling. I will be honest and clear without feeling like I am burdening them.
3. Find flow, non-resistance by consciously choosing not to be so serious and pessimistic.
   I will bring back creative activity into my life starting with painting. I love to paint. This optimistic and enjoyable activity will distract my mind and is a conscious choice not to focus on what's wrong in my life, to stop focusing on the negative.
4. I will carry clear quartz with me in my purse to clear out my personal energy and help me feel happier.

Thunder Trigram

Intention:
My intention is to live in the light expanding energy of thunder; to live as a powerful person who brings release and freedom to situations and to others.

Affirmation:
I am inspirational and I am powerful and free and I choose to create safe, strong connections. I reprogram myself towards the light expanding energy of thunder and I breathe in connection and I breathe out disconnection. I breathe in acceptance and I breathe out forcing.

Light expanding thunder energy:
Q: Where in your life do you feel your power? Power that makes things happen, brings order and structure, creates outcomes?

A: Powerful? I am so far from feeling powerful! I used to feel powerful. I used to feel my power in my personality and in the way I could make things happen. Now it seems that I'm going through the motions, just coping with the day to day. This question makes me see that I am really just allowing life to buffet me around, I'm not guiding my life anymore. I know that I feel helpless in the chaos that I'm experiencing, that I feel that life is happening to me. But I also see that I could take back some control, feel some strength. Maybe. That feels powerful.

Q: Light expanding thunder energy is being non-judgmental, broad minded, seeing all perspectives. Is this part of your life?

A: This question makes me feel good as I see that even as I have collapsed into my dark energy, I am still able to live in a way that is non-judgmental towards others. I still have great compassion for the lives of others. I guess the perspective that I have not been able to see is mainly focused on my life. I haven't had a perspective of hope — not lately.

Q: What healthy connections do you have with others?

A: My family and inner circle are really important connections to me.

I wonder how healthy they are when I don't share my fears with them? Most of the time I try to hide how worried I am from them. I am torn between understanding the need for open communication; and not wanting to give my fears more energy by talking about them. I wonder how healthy my connections actually are?

Q: How is your thunder energy helping those around you? How does your desire to be of service and help others show up?

A: Everyone I love knows that I am there for them. I am certain of that. Unquestioned.

Dark collapsed thunder energy:
Note to myself – remember to use the third person talk to help me get a bit more objectivity.

Q: Which part of the dark thunder energy is Brenda experiencing now:

A: Brenda is experiencing "feel the world is a dangerous place 'and "feeling unsafe, feeling at risk". This is about Brenda losing her job.

A: Brenda is also experiencing "it should be something else". This is about the ill health of her loved ones.

Q: What would life be like if Brenda could turn this around and reprogram towards the light expanding energy of thunder?

A: Brenda has felt so weak lately. Light thunder energy is exactly the opposite of weak. There has been so much resistance to what is going on in Brenda's life that she hasn't seen thunder energy as bringing rain, relief and nourishment, but rather thunder energy that is dangerous and brings bad things. Brenda is ready to take back her power.

I AM POWERFUL!

I AM FREE!

Dear Higher Self

Please bring me wisdom and understanding. Please help me reach for the power within me again.

Let me find myself again. I have been so focused and overwhelmed by the troubles that life has thrown at me, that I forgot I have power inside.

Antidote and Action:

1. Connect with others, find ways to be of service.
   I will follow up with my friend. She asked me to help her with a project that assists young women. I had resisted this as I was so preoccupied with myself. I will help some-one else.
2. Balance your life by getting rid of all the 'shoulds' – for yourself and for others.
   I will do my very best to allow life to happen. It is what it is. (This one is going to be very difficult for me, but I guess even having the awareness is a good step!)
3. Find flow, non-resistance by accepting others and build-ing strong foundations for relationships.
   I will strengthen my relationships by finding a way to be honest with my loved ones about how I'm feeling.
4. I will carry jade with me in my purse to help give me clarity.

Heaven Trigram

Intention:
My intention is to live in the light expanding energy of heaven; to live as a supported and expanding person who feels mighty and unrestricted.

Affirmation:
I am supported and expanding and I choose to feel supported. I reprogram myself towards the light expanding energy of heaven and I breathe in support and I breathe out rejection. I breathe in unrestricted creation and I breathe out self pity.

Light expanding heaven energy:
Q: How does the creation energy of heaven show up in your life? Do you ever feel mighty and unrestricted? Where? with whom? When?

A: Wow! Just reading the words mighty and unrestricted tell me how far I've fallen from my normal state of mind. I feel very far away from 'mighty and unrestricted' but it wasn't so long ago that I did feel mighty and unrestricted. My thoughts slide back so easily to my fears. With both the illness of my loved one and my job loss — I feel so out of control. That's a million miles away from mighty and unrestricted. Heaven as a concept is very helpful in putting life into perspective. I guess I need to focus the creation energy of heaven onto myself.

Q: Is your life balanced between being physically active and spiritually connected?

A: No, is my answer. Only if doing nothing physically and feeling spiritually disconnected also represents balance. (That's a bit of sic humour!) Whenever life gets too heavy I stop exercising – this feels like a good time to get moving again. This journaling with the Daily Pulse is helping me regain my spiritual connection.

Q: Are you good at both giving and receiving support – or is there an imbalance there? What could you do about that?

A: I seem to have withdrawn from life – neither giving nor receiving support. What to do?

I have decided to help my friend with her young women's project. Now I just have to get good at receiving support – somehow that feels more difficult. I will keep the thought in my meditations and prayers.

Q: What is your perspective on the meaning of life?

A: Slowly it is starting to feel better, as I work through these Daily Pulse exercises and regain the understanding that there is nothing in my life that I can't cope with. Slowly I am seeing a bigger picture perspective.

In a way, what have I got to lose? I just can't go on with how I'm feeling now - feeling small and limited – instead of mighty and unrestricted.

It's not like this is the first time I've had big things to deal with – it's just that my response to life has been so fearful this time.

Dark collapsed heaven energy:
Note to myself – remember to use the third person talk to help me get a bit more objectivity.

Q: Which part of the dark heaven energy is Brenda experiencing now:

A: Brenda is experiencing "Being unable to give your life context, to see the big picture, to have a broader view point, your frame of reference is too small with mostly a negative aspect". Brenda is sometimes so full of fear!

Q: What would life be like if Brenda could turn this around and reprogram towards the light expanding energy of heaven?

A: Brenda would feel strong and capable again. Brenda would be able to say I AM MIGHTY AND UNRESTRICED! And really mean it.

Dear Higher Self

Thank you for helping me to have a better perspective on what is going on in my life. Please help me make these occasional glimpses more frequent. Please help me find ways to reconnect with the mighty and unrestricted part of me. She's in there somewhere – help me find her again.

Antidote and Action:

1. Connect with others by giving support and receiving support.
   I will give support to younger women working alongside my friend. Next time someone offers to help me, I will say yes.
2. Balance your life by focusing on a bigger perspective.
   I will create reminders to myself about the bigger perspective of life. Remembering that there is more to life than these everyday worries is really good for me. It's just that I forget when I go down my fear spirals. Reminders on my phone will be helpful.
3. Find flow, non-resistance by consciously choosing to collaborate with others, to participate and be inclusive.
   I will keep the creation energy of heaven, and the possibility of feeling mighty and unrestricted in my conscious awareness.
4. I will carry smoky quartz with me in my purse to bring me serenity and help connect me to my higher self, my soul. (My purse is getting full!)

<u>Water Trigram</u>

Intention:
My intention is to live in the light expanding energy of water; to live as a deep person who flows through life, one who understands non-resistance and lives with quiet reflection.

Affirmation:
I am compassionate and I am confident and deep and I choose to feel accepted. I reprogram myself towards the light expanding energy of water and I breathe in being decisive and I breathe out indecision. I breathe in assurance and I breathe out uncertainty.

Light expanding water energy:
Q: Do you know what it feels like to focus on a goal and flow downstream? What happens when you do? How can you bring more of that into your life now?

A: My goal at the moment is for my loved one to get better! I just had a big aha! moment. This goal is completely unrealistic – it's all about me with nothing about my loved one.

My goal should be for them to have the perfect life experience that they desire (at a conscious, sub-conscious and unconscious or soul level) and that includes any ill health that they wrote into their soul plan.

This goal of mine is complete and utter resistance to our life together and the big picture! I'm not sure what to do with this new understanding, but I will ask in the Higher Self section for help.

Q: Do you ever feel confident and assured? When you feel so good that you share your journey and quest for meaning in life?

A: Once again — I used to feel confident and assured. I used to have lovely deep conversations with others about the meaning of life. My life has just got so small and fearful that I don't think I've had a meaningful conversation for ages.

I have withdrawn from my friends because I don't want to talk about my troubles — I have this weird suspicion that talking about them makes them bigger. But I miss the deep conversations and I can have them again if I choose to. I do choose to.

Q: Would you define your relationships as healthy, with boundaries?

A: No, not if my goals are interfering with my loved ones life experiences! Yikes — not sure what to do with this understanding.

Q: What does a life of flow and non-resistance feel like? Why can't you have more of that?

A: A life of flow and non-resistance would include accepting that this sickness that has overtaken us and losing my job are all part of life. That I am taken care of by spirit and why could this all not be the start of something great? A life of flow and non-resistance feels like peace and calm and reassurance and satisfaction and confidence and soothe.

Dark collapsed water energy:
Note to myself – remember to use the third person talk to help me get a bit more objectivity.

Q: Which part of the dark water energy is Brenda experiencing now:

A: Brenda is experiencing "feel overwhelmed, flow everywhere and flow nowhere". This is about Brenda feeling helpless about her loved ones ill health.

A: Brenda is also experiencing "your negative emotions about your-self are your gloomy interpretation". This is about Brenda losing her job.

Q: What would life be like if Brenda could turn this around and reprogram towards the light expanding energy of water?

A: Brenda could choose to embody water energy – to feel deep, calm and still – that would be a nice change. She has al-lowed her emotions to overflow, be destructive and have no boundaries.

Dear Higher Self

Please help me understand the role that this sickness is playing in our lives. Please help me accept that all is well. Please help me find non-resistance. How do I wish for them to get better while not interfering with their experience? Please show me the way.

Antidote and Action:

1. Connect with others to create healthy boundaries.
   I will reconnect with my friends for those lovely deep conversations that we used to enjoy.
2. Balance your life by choosing to feel accepted.
   I will find balance in my life by accepting the situation as it is – just as it is – even though it is not what I want. I can do this!
3. Find flow, non-resistance by focusing on a goal, taking the next best step and flowing downstream.
   I will focus on flowing downstream, on taking one step at a time, on finding non-resistance. I can also do this!
4. I will carry onyx with me in my purse to help build my inner strength.

Mountain Trigram

Intention:
My intention is to live in the light expanding energy of mountain; to live as a strong, steady and wise person who has faith and chooses to trust life.

Affirmation:
I am spiritual and I am strong, steady and wise and I choose to relax and trust. I reprogram myself towards the light expanding energy of mountain and I breathe in trust and I breathe out distrust. I breathe in hope and I breathe out doubt.

Light expanding mountain energy:
Q: What does it feel like to be connected to your innate wisdom?

A: That feels like a distant memory! Being connected to my innate wisdom is so many feelings - all of which become the single word, love. Loving the journey, loving the experience, loving what is happening. Even this difficult stuff, especially this difficult stuff.

Q: What would a life based on faith and trust be like?

A: Just how do I find this faith and trust?!!? Because that life looks incredible. That life looks peaceful. That life looks secure.

Sorry about this, but today I'm just feeling sorry for myself. Sorry about the situation, feeling that this is all NOT FAIR! Sorry that

I have lost myself in my anxiety and fear. Just plain SORRY! It's all very well to ask 'what would a life based on faith and trust be like' but how do I find that????

Q: Are you taking the time to explore beliefs and intangibles and then share them with others?

A: No. That has all fallen by the wayside. But thinking about reading a new and exciting spiritual book makes me feel more calm. I love taking spiritual courses online and haven't done that for ages.

Answering these Daily Pulse questions has really made me see how I have let the so called 'bad' things in my life overtake my whole life. I can change that for sure.

Q: Mountain energy is firmly rooted to earth and reaches up to the heavens. What does this mean for you in your life?

A: It means that I can take it all, all that life throws at me. Because I have a firm rooting in my life on earth; I have a solid and strong base just like a mountain. And I also have a great connection to my higher self, my soul and God because just like the mountain I reach up to heaven.

Mountain energy is the connection between heaven and earth. I believe that I have a connection to heaven and earth.

Dark collapsed mountain energy:
Note to myself – remember to use the third person talk to help me
get a bit more objectivity.

Q: Which part of the dark mountain energy is Brenda experiencing now:

A: Brenda is experiencing "life isn't fair". Brenda is also experiencing "lack of faith and not trusting the process of life".

Q: What would life be like if Brenda could turn this around and
reprogram towards the light expanding energy of mountain?

A: Brenda knows she has innate wisdom. She is being reminded
of it as she works through the Daily Pulse. Brenda is remembering what she always knew – that life will work out for the best,
that she is strong and steady, that she can reach for peace and
hope. Faith is a choice. Trust is a choice. Can Brenda choose faith
and trust? She has no other choice really because the worry and
anxiety that have been her constant companions are not the way
she wants to live anymore. You can do it Brenda!

Dear Higher Self

Please remind me how to strengthen my faith that life will work
out. Please show me how to trust this experience.

Please be with me all the way.

I ask that you bring me inspiration about solutions, about practical things that I can do to find my faith and trust again. Thank you.

Antidote and Action:

1. *Connect with others by 'walking in their shoes'.*
   I will try to take the focus off me and put some focus on others who are having a hard time. I will stop the constant agonizing about my life's difficulties and remember others too.
2. *Balance your life by focusing on your spiritual connection and being constant, certain and strong.*
   I will find an online spiritual course to enjoy.
3. *Find flow, non-resistance by consciously choosing to have faith and trust in the flow of life.*
   I will regularly meditate and diligently say my prayers, asking for help with this.
4. *I will carry lapis lazuli with me in my purse to help promote my connection to spirit.*

Wind Trigram

Intention:
My intention is to live in the light expanding energy of wind; to live as a kind, gentle, curious and connected person who uses their inner power and energy to make life better.

Affirmation:
I am intellectual and I am curious and connected and I choose to be kind. I reprogram myself towards the light expanding energy of wind and I breathe in generosity and I breathe out withholding. I breathe in kindness and I breathe out restriction.

Light expanding wind energy:
Q: What happens in your life when you are generous and share your blessings?

A: It feels like it would be a relief to share something with others. I have been so myopic and focused on my own 'troubles'. Part of me has felt like there wasn't any additional energy to share with others, that I just had to keep to myself, to protect myself. But I see that not sharing with others hasn't worked. I will make a real effort to reach out.

Q: Do you feel your inner power and energy? How do you use it?

A: Nope. I used to.

But I see that if I take all of the actions that I have committed to

– that I will feel my inner power again. I already sense a difference with some of the things I have introduced into my life. This Daily Pulse journaling is making me see my own power again. Very grateful.

Q: When do you feel supercharged with strong personal chi? With whom? Why is that?

A: I am reaching for this. I am reaching for this feeling. I know it's deep inside me and that I will be able to find it. I am very familiar with my supercharged self, she just got lost along the way. Today I feel confident that I will find her again.

Q: Wind creates change, it is cleansing and cooling. Do you see those characteristics in your life?

A: I took the steps to feel better. I am still taking the steps and doing the work to feel better. That's change. Yes, I do see the cleansing and cooling characteristics of wind in my life. Well done me! This is a great change.

Dark collapsed wind energy:
Note to myself – remember to use the third person talk to help me get a bit more objectivity.

Q: Which part of the dark wind energy is Brenda experiencing now:

A: Brenda is experiencing "negative emotions are described as the wind that blows out the lamp of the mind." And "feeling helpless under external controls".

Q: What would life be like if Brenda could turn this around and reprogram towards the light expanding energy of wind?

A: In this trigram Brenda is really seeing that change is possible and that she is making progress towards feeling better. Her natural nature is to be kind and generous. She just pulled into herself when the catastrophes happened. So close together. So intense. But it's time for Brenda to make things better for herself and for her loved ones.

It's time for her to embrace the wind that can blow all her cares away and feels like angel's breath.

Dear Higher Self

Thank you, I am feeling better. I feel as if I am taking my life back. I feel more able to cope. Guide me to live in light expanding energy, help me to choose my light especially when the news about my loved ones or my job hunt is not good. I remain curious and connected to you.

Antidote and Action:

1. Connect with others by sharing and being kind. I can do this. It is my nature. It is easy for me. I had just forgotten to do this.

2. Balance your life by focusing on your curiosity and connection.

   I will stay curious and I will encourage my connection to spirit with a regular meditation practice. I love meditating and this will give me a beautiful focus for this time to be with myself.

3. Find flow, non-resistance by consciously including and accepting others. By sharing your blessings.

   I will reach out to others again. I feel like a tortoise that is peeking her head out of her shell. It feels cautious and it also feels familiar.

4. I will carry amethyst with me in my purse to promote clear thinking.

Tai Chi energy

Intention:
My intention is to live in the light expanding energy of the tai chi; to live a life that is balanced, flowing, peaceful and tranquil.

Affirmation:
I know my life's plan, I am happy and whole and I choose to be allowing. I reprogram myself towards the light expanding energy of the tai chi and I breathe in allowing and I breathe out resistance. I breathe in flow and I breathe out struggle.

Light expanding tai chi energy:
Q: What does the perspective that balance is created internally mean to you and your life?

A: I certainly have not been experiencing mental steadiness nor emotional stability during this difficult time. But I am feeling more tranquil and peaceful as I have worked through the Daily Pulse. It has really given me perspective again and that has created internal balance for me.

Q: If balance is a state of being, what could you do differently?

A: I can stop holding onto what I can't control and I can let go of some of the fears that are causing my negative emotional state.

I can remind myself to allow life to be what it is, to reach for hope. It is inside of me – I can find it.

Q: How can you find your inner calm? What are you doing to move your life forward?

A: It's coming back. It's beautiful. I found it deep inside and each day it is becoming clearer and easier to find. I am moving my life forward by doing this work. By asking for help. By committing to take the action suggested. I am doing it.

Q: Rhythm and ritual create balance, how can you make your Daily Pulse part of your life going forward?

A: I will reach for my tools. I will read the intention for the trigrams, complete a breath prayer twice a day, continue with journaling and my meditations and prayers. I will also compile a complete list of all that I have contracted to do for my antidote and actions, so that I can move towards the accomplishing of that and find my way towards the light of each trigram.

Dark collapsed tai chi energy:
Note to myself – remember to use the third person talk to help me get a bit more objectivity.

Q: Which part of the dark tai chi energy is Brenda experiencing now:

A: Brenda is experiencing "looking for balance outside of you" and "understanding the balance between what you can control and what you cannot control; living between resistance and surrender".

Brenda has felt significant resistance to both losing her job and the sickness that has become such an big part of her life.

Q: What would life be like if Brenda could turn this around and reprogram towards the light expanding energy of tai chi?

A: Brenda now understands that finding hope comes from changing what is happening inside of her. Feeling acceptance brings balance.

Putting her experiences into perspective, understanding that life is a soul experience, all of this helps her to feel more balanced. Brenda has experienced that synchronizing with the Tao and bringing the rhythm and ritual of the Daily Pulse into her life has indeed helped her to feel happier again.

Dear Higher Self

Thank you for being on this journey with me. I have felt you help me find solutions and I have felt my peace and calm return. Please be with me on those days when I don't feel balanced. Help me to remember that I know how to find it again.

Help me to be consistent with my Daily Pulse, keeping up with the rhythm and ritual that has been so transformational. Thank you.

Antidote and Action:

1. Connect with others by allowing them their life experience, allowing them to be who they are.

    This is for me. I will allow myself to be human and flow through this difficult life experience. On those days when I am not feeling balanced, I will reach for my tools and let them quietly and gently restore my peace and calm.

2. Balance your life by focusing on living with balance and emotional steadiness.

    I will reach for my tools. I will find ways to soothe myself. I remember how to do this now.

3. Find flow, non-resistance by consciously choosing to introduce rhythm and ritual into your life. Creating a daily habit of pulse, sanctuary and connection.

    Dr. Debra always says that it's all very well to know about the tools, but if you don't reach into your tool bag and grab the one you need — they aren't going to help. I promise myself that I will keep up this daily practice. I will continue to find a quiet time each day to be with myself.

4. I will carry citrine with me in my purse to balance and heal me physically, mentally and emotionally.

APPENDIX II – COMPLETE INTENTION AND AFFIRMATION LIST

Intention:
To live in the light expanding energy of fire; to live as a clear, warm, bright and enlightened person who has courage and leads by example.

Affirmation:
I am charismatic and I am bright and aware and I choose to be true to myself. I reprogram myself towards the light expanding energy of fire and I breathe in growth and I breathe out fear. I breathe in courage and I breathe out feeling small.

EARTH TRIGRAM

Intention:
To live in the light expanding energy of earth; to live as a nourishing and nourished person who keeps a sense of self in relationships.

Affirmation:
I know who I am, I am important and significant and I choose to feel valued. I reprogram myself towards the light expanding energy of earth and I breathe in worthiness and I breathe out unworthiness. I breathe in nourishment and I breathe out sacrifice.

LAKE TRIGRAM

Intention:
To live in the light expanding energy of lake; to live as a positive, full and fun person who is creative and full of ideas and imagination.

Affirmation:
I am intuitive and I am fun and full and I choose to have fun. I reprogram myself towards the light expanding energy of lake and I breathe in positivity and I breathe out pessimism. I breathe in happiness and I breathe out negativity.

THUNDER TRIGRAM

Intention:
To live in the light expanding energy of thunder; to live as a powerful person who brings release and freedom to situations and to others.

Affirmation:
I am inspirational and I am powerful and free and I choose to create safe, strong connections. I reprogram myself towards the light expanding energy of thunder and I breathe in connection and I breathe out disconnection. I breathe in acceptance and I breathe out forcing.

HEAVEN TRIGRAM

Intention:
To live in the light expanding energy of heaven; to live as a supported and expanding person who feels mighty and unrestricted.

Affirmation:
I am supported and expanding and I choose to feel supported. I reprogram myself towards the light expanding energy of heaven and I breathe in support and I breathe out rejection. I breathe in unrestricted creation and I breathe out self pity.

WATER TRIGRAM

Intention:
To live in the light expanding energy of water; to live as a deep person who flows through life, one who understands non-resistance and lives with quiet reflection.

Affirmation:
I am compassionate and I am confident and deep and I choose to feel accepted. I reprogram myself towards the light expanding energy of water and I breathe in being decisive and I breathe out indecision. I breathe in assurance and I breathe out uncertainty.

MOUNTAIN TRIGRAM

Intention:
To live in the light expanding energy of mountain; to live as a strong, steady and wise person who has faith and chooses to trust life.

Affirmation:
I am spiritual and I am strong, steady and wise and I choose to relax and trust. I reprogram myself towards the light expanding energy of mountain and I breathe in trust and I breathe out distrust. I breathe in hope and I breathe out doubt.

WIND TRIGRAM

Intention:
To live in the light expanding energy of wind; to live as a kind, gentle, curious and connected person who uses their inner power and energy to make life better.

Affirmation:
I am intellectual and I am curious and connected and I choose to be kind. I reprogram myself towards the light expanding energy of wind and I breathe in generosity and I breathe out withholding. I breathe in kindness and I breathe out restriction.

· · ● ● ● · ● ● ● · ● ● ● · ● ●

TAI CHI ENERGY

Intention:
To live in the light expanding energy of the tai chi; to live a life that is balanced, flowing, peaceful and tranquil.

Affirmation:
I know my life's plan, I am happy and whole and I choose to be allowing. I reprogram myself towards the light expanding energy of the tai chi and I breathe in allowing and I breathe out resistance. I breathe in flow and I breathe out struggle.

· · ● ● ● · ● ● ● · ● ● ● · ● ●

DAILY PULSE
The rhythm of the Tao

BOOKS BY DR. DEBRA FORD

Available on **Amazon.com**

1. **Divination of the Tao, book of wisdom (2019)**

   The answers to questions are always available when you access the wisdom of your soul or higher self. Divination is a way to access guidance by connecting to that part of you that is 'more than your physical body'. Divination brings to your conscious awareness guidance that helps you find answers. Answers, which at a deeper level, you already know.

   The divination guidance in this book of wisdom is based on the profound beauty of the Tao. The Tao is the natural order of the universe and the Tao keeps the world balanced and flowing.

2. **Emilia Rose and the rainbow adventure. Book 1 in the series 'the adventures of Emilia Rose and the LiaBots', stories for children based on the profound beauty of the Tao (2019)**

   Emilia Rose had a secret, one that she didn't share with anyone. Her secret was that each night in her dreams she travelled to LiaLand and lived among the friendly, funny, cheeky and brave LiaBots.

One night, Emilia Rose was in her LiaLand dream and saw a rainbow. Rainbows just made her smile, they were so pretty. "Where do they come from?" she wondered. "I know" she said, "The LiaBots can solve this mystery for me". They were to go on an adventure, out into the world and find out where rainbows begin.

This is the first of Emilia Rose's adventures with the LiaBots and is based on the key understandings of the Tao:

1. Connection – between us all and also with everything
2. Balance – when one part is out of balance, all are affected
3. Flow – non-resistance to what is going on around you

Three principles that our children seem to understand intuitively.

3. Daily Pulse, the rhythm of the Tao (2018)

Starting and ending each ay with deliberate choices creates calm. A daily ritual becomes a regular habit to provide rhythm and peace to everyday. The Daily Pulse is a ritual based on the profound beauty of the Tao.

The Daily Pulse helps you take small steps towards transformation, towards happiness. The Daily Pulse encourages you to see beyond the ache and disorientation of life's challenges, to being normalcy and ritual to everyday.

4. SolePath the path to purpose and a beautiful life (2013)

'This book is the story of SolePath and of Debra's ability to hear the teachings of SolePath. She models for others how this can be done. So that those who read this book are inspired towards their own body of work; the great truth that will be theirs.' Seth

1. **The Tao and the SolePath categories (2015)**

    The Tao forms the foundation for all of our work, including SoleNumbers, SoleFaces, SoleHealing and of course the beautiful body of work called SolePath. The Tao represents the fundamental nature of the universe, the origin, the creator. The Tao means your path or your life's journey. The Tao is the understanding of life, an awareness of that which cannot be fully grasped. A belief in that which cannot be fully explained – but is known by the soul.

2. **The Tao and the LightPaths (2015)**

    Your two LightPaths are a place of expanded energy. They are who you are born to be and provide clues to your purpose, to your gifts and greatness.

    LightPaths are how you discover the 'thing' that you are born to do and have the life experience your soul intended. When you live your life from your LightPath expansion you find joy, health, love, happiness and meaning. You also learn how you can serve and make a difference in the world.

3. The Tao and the DarkPath (2015)

Your DarkPath is a place of collapsed energy. It is mastered energy and is believed to have been completed in a past lifetime. You have lived your DarkPath in a different life and bring all of the skills of this path into this lifetime. Your DarkPath therefore feels easy for you, automatic, almost your deepest sub-conscious response, but it does not have any of the excitement, joy and purpose of your LightPaths. Your DarkPath is therefore often more familiar than your LightPaths.

4. The Tao and SoleNumbers (2015)

SoleNumbers answers the question 'what am I doing here?' SoleNumbers helps you understand that there are two purposes for your life. Firstly, an inward purpose, an inward journey for your soul that relates to your own, unique, personal life experience. Secondly, an outward purpose, an understanding of 'what I am meant to be doing with my life' and what the impact of that will be on others with whom you connect consciously and energetically.

5. The Tao and SoleFaces (2015)

Your face provides clues to the habits and behaviours that are holding you back from living in your greatness. Your face shows the blocks that stop you from being who you are born to be and what you are meant to be doing with your life. Your face is the road map of your life experiences. Your face is the story of where you have been and who you have been. Your face shows the impact of others in your life. Your face is the truest indication of your limiting beliefs and behaviours that have brought you to this moment. *'SoleFaces is about habit. It is about habitual behaviour that leads you down the rabbit hole, in relationships, in behaviour, in workplaces. SoleFaces is the patterns and habits that have brought you to here.'* Seth

6. The Tao and SoleHealing (2015)

Revelation #1: *'Within each person there is a vibration that can be matched for perfect health.' Seth.*

Revelation #2: You can only heal your body when you are experiencing expanded energy.

Revelation #3: Negative emotion is the cause of your mental and physical dis-ease. *'A SoleHealing diagnosis identifies energetic blocks and provides direction for healing.' Seth* The SoleHealing diagnosis includes a three-part treatment plan for your health and healing.

7. The Tao and SoleIntending (2015)

This book is a profoundly simple concept that connects the fundamental teachings of the Tao to a balanced intending process to create the life of your dreams.

8. The Tao and Emotional Divination (2015)

The purpose of this book is moving you from dark to light; from collapsed negative energy to expanding positive energy. It is about finding your way in life, being happier and making a difference one person at a time.

9. The 180 of Intention (2014)

A transcript of an incredible conversation between Seth and Liz about the new energy on our planet, creating our lives, and the new 180 energy of intention.

10. In the Feng Shui Zone (2005)

A tried and tested ancient Chinese art and science to effect improvements in your life. A practical, simple and easy to follow process that includes a 9-step guide to getting your home and your life into the zone. A new approach to Feng Shui based on our western living style and the beautiful foundation of the Tao.

ABOUT THE AUTHOR

Dr. Debra is a spiritual philosophy teacher with a doctorate in metaphysical science. She is an ordained minister and a member of the American metaphysical doctors association and the Canadian international metaphysical ministry.

Dr. Debra's SolePath is inspirational teacher and spiritual mystic. It is this SolePath that allows her to connect, create and communicate the SolePath body of work. She is the author of 16 books including *"SolePath the path to purpose and a beautiful life"* and *"Daily Pulse, rhythm of the Tao"*. Her core values and core energy are spirituality and connection, inspiration and communication.

Dr. Debra Ford is the co-founder of the SolePath Institute, along with the four core team of John Ford, Deneen Justason and Terry Justason. The SolePath Institute joyfully encourages everyone to know and understand their SolePath and live a beautiful life, filled with purpose and meaning. The SolePath Institute provides support and guidance on your journey, helping you to take the next best step.

SOLEPATH INSTITUTE

WHAT IS SOLEPATH?

> *"SolePath is who you are born to be. It is your guide to a beautiful life, filled with happiness, peace, joy, love, purpose and meaning. When you know your SolePath, you can navigate the pitfalls and those things that trip you up in your life, and connect with your unique, personal, individual gifts and greatness."* Dr. Debra

SolePath is your soul ID. At the Calgary SolePath Institute we measure your energetics and give you your best lifehack ever, your SolePath. When you know your SolePath you can be who you dreamed you'd be and who the world needs you to be.

Your SolePath helps you find your role so that you can make a difference because as Plato said "there is a place that you are to fill and no one else can fill. Something that you are to do, which no one else can do."

Your SolePath is a braid of two LightPaths and one DarkPath. Your LightPaths are expanding energy and provide direction for knowing your life's purpose; your DarkPath is collapsed energy and provides contrast for personal growth.

Knowing your SolePath is priceless but you pay only what you feel able to give. The SolePath Institute vision is for everyone to know their SolePath and that is why all SolePath readings are by donation.

Request your SolePath at **www.SolePath.org** You will be asked to upload a headshot selfie and fill out a short form with some identifying information. It can take up to 5 days to complete your SolePath reading, although we do try really hard to be quicker. You will receive your results by email and also be booked for a face-to-face debrief, either in person or by Skype.

"SolePath is always only about you, about you as an individual finding your way and walking your path to purpose and a beautiful life." Dr. Debra

Websites: www.DailyPulse.ca
                   www.SolePathInstitute.org

Email: **answers@SolePath.org**

Mailing address: SolePath Institute,
1329 8th Avenue SE, Inglewood
Calgary Alberta T2G 0M8
Canada

Helpline: 403.998.0191
1.877.866.2086

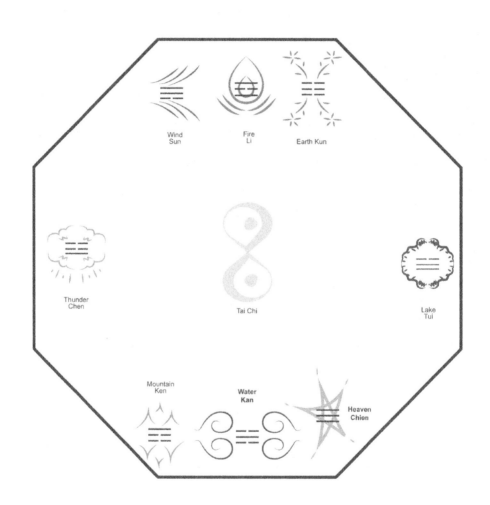

Wind
Sun

Fire
Li

Earth Kun

Thunder
Chen

Tai Chi

Lake
Tui

Mountain
Ken

Water
Kan

Heaven
Chien

Made in the USA
Monee, IL
05 April 2020

24540652R00105